God of Chance

David J. Bartholomew

SCM PRESS LTD

Bartholomew, David J.
  God of chance.
  1. Chance
  I. Title
  261.5'1   BD595

  ISBN 0-334-02030-1

First published 1984
by SCM Press Ltd
26–30 Tottenham Road, London N1

Photoset by The Spartan Press Limited
Lymington, Hants
and printed in Great Britain by
Richard Clay (The Chaucer Press) Ltd
Bungay, Suffolk

God of Chance

CONTENTS

AUTHOR'S NOTE

A book which spans so many disciplines requires the reader's indulgence on two counts. First, although it is the peculiar attraction of statistical science that it gains entry for its practitioners to so many fields this does not guarantee expertise. It is inevitable that my excursions into the territory of others will betray incomplete and, perhaps, inaccurate understanding but I am optimistic that such blemishes will not seriously detract from the main thesis. Secondly, for those not trained in quantitative matters, the resort to a formal style of argument, principally in Chapter 3, may cause difficulty. The matter has been kept as simple as possible and the treatment is self-contained but the reader unfamiliar with this mode of reasoning must expect to take things very slowly. As we shall see, one can easily go astray by trying to avoid the precision which mathematical reasoning imposes. But even if these passages are skipped I believe the general thrust of the argument will be clear.

All biblical references are to the New English Bible, unless otherwise stated.

ACKNOWLEDGMENTS

It is all too easy to imagine that the ideas of others, absorbed long ago, are one's own. My own interest in the relationship between science and religion goes back to hearing the late Professor C. A. Coulson speak on various occasions in the 1950s, though as far as I can remember he never dealt directly with the role of chance. It has been nourished since by the writings of many of those referred to in the following pages whose influence and stimulation I am glad to acknowledge.

My wife, Marian, has added to her other roles that of typist and general assistant and to her my thanks cannot be better expressed than in the words of Proverbs 19.14 (NEB).

1

God and Chance

A preview

Chance has come to play a fundamental role in scientific thinking. This fact poses questions for theology which are only now beginning to be fully appreciated and to which the answers are far from clear. The older and simpler picture of the universe as a vast well-oiled machine obeying immutable laws has given way to something much more complex and subtle. It was difficult enough to see how God might be able to break the laws of nature to perform miracles. The very lawfulness of nature almost seemed to imprison God within his own creation. Now the challenge comes from the opposite direction. The theologian has to explain how God could be conceived of as acting purposefully in a world where the driving force appears to be chance – the very antithesis of purpose. In a sense the wheel has come full circle. Before the scientific revolution events were commonly supposed to be in the hands of capricious deities; unpredictability was the hallmark of experience. Now the gods have been dethroned but the uncertainty remains.

It was recognized quite early that some of the laws of science were statistical in the sense that they described the average effects of large numbers of small scale events. The kinetic theory of gases, for example, could explain Boyle's law in terms of the chaotic movement of the molecules of a gas. But later, with the discovery that there appeared to be an irreducible uncertainty at the heart of matter, chance entered science in a more fundamental way. Now, in the aftermath of Darwin's evolutionary theory, chance plays an even wider role; natural selection works on chance variation which is rooted in a randomness in the mechanism of heredity. It could thus be claimed, with some justice, that uncertainty rather than order is the characteristic of science.

Christian history spans all of these stages. Theologians have scarcely recovered from one assault on their positions by science than the next has been upon them. It says much for the vitality and toughness of religious faith that it has survived those onslaughts in reasonably good order. There have, of course, been numerical losses in the West where the scientific mode of thought has penetrated most deeply but even so there is no lack of people who combine a scientific understanding and a deep faith without compromising their integrity. However, faith and theology are not the same thing and it is the latter which is having to be radically re-structured. The earliest conflict concerning Galileo's espousal of the Copernican theory soon passed, but the reverberations from Darwin's theory have not yet completely died away. However, in both cases it was the direct challenge to the authority of the Bible, rather than the less obvious implications for the way God works, which seems to have been largely responsible for the furore. The fact that the quantum theory did not directly threaten the literal truth of the Bible may account for the more muted reception with which its implications have been received by theologians. Similarly the very serious challenge to conceptions of God's providence posed by the findings of evolutionary genetics has not shaken the foundations of belief as much as its importance might have led one to expect. The idea, so eloquently advocated by Jacques Monod,[1] that there is no direction behind evolution but that all is the result of 'pure, blind chance', strikes at the root of belief in a purposeful God. This amounts, Monod believed, to a virtual disproof of almost all that religion stands for. If it is really true that chance is so fundamental a characteristic of the world, it is not easy to see how one could persist in belief in a providential God. Can theism, and Christianity in particular, be saved without emasculating it to the point where it ceases to mean anything significant? Monod has set up what might be called a 'natural anti-theology'. Is there a natural theology which, while giving full weight to scientific knowledge, can re-establish the integrity of the Christian position?

Natural theology is somewhat out of favour, but if the case against Christian theism is not to go by default an attempt must be made to re-colonize the lost territory. This book is written in the belief that the role of chance in the scheme of things is both real and fundamental and therefore that a serious attempt must be made to accommodate it within a theistic framework. It is not the first such attempt, of course, and we shall have frequent cause to draw on the work of our predecessors. But there have been very few who have made chance their main focus and none, so far as I am aware, for whom chance, in the shape of probability theory and statistics was their main professional concern.

There is one strand of probabilistic thinking which has caught the notice of philosophical theologians, though it stands apart from the main literature of science and religion. It runs counter to the current of thinking which we have outlined above. In its simplest form it asserts that what has occurred in the world is so extremely improbable that chance, as an explanation must be ruled out. The most recent exponents of this idea are Hoyle and Wickramasinghe,[2] but it goes back to the eighteenth century. Behind this line of reasoning is the common misapprehension that we have to choose between God and chance as two mutually exclusive explanations. To those who see things in these terms the present enterprise is doomed from the start. If such people take a theistic position it appears to them that chance is virtually synonymous with atheism since it implies the absence of any intention or purpose. To admit such purposeless activity would be to impugn the sovereignty of God if not actually to deny his existence. This view does not, among its more sophisticated adherents, at least, rule out the use of probability theory in science. The latter is seen merely as a formal way of expressing our ignorance. If we were capable of seeing things as God sees them, the argument goes, all uncertainty would vanish. Attractive though this view may seem it tends to a determinism which, if pressed too far, abolishes human freedom and so reduces us to mere automata.

It would be a mistake to gain the impression that the 'God or chance' dilemma can be so easily dismissed. There are cogent arguments which make it the starting point for a proof of God's existence. Although we shall ultimately find this wanting, it has been rather too easily dismissed by writers on the 'proofs' for the existence of God. Chapter 3 is devoted to an examination of the logic of the argument in the various forms in which it has been advanced. This subject is important not only for its intrinsic interest but also because, if the argument were valid, it would demolish Monod's case at a stroke. Monod maintained that chance was responsible for the way things are. Hoyle and his predecessors claim that this cannot be true. It should be noted that probability considerations enter here in two ways which must be clearly distinguished. First, they arise in a technical way in the calculation of the probabilities of the events in question; secondly, in a logical sense, when we come to measure the degree of credibility to be attached to inductive inferences. This alerts us to the need to be careful about terminology and especially about such words as 'chance', 'randomness' and 'probability'. We shall take up such questions later. In the meantime the everyday connotations of the words must suffice because it is first necessary to build up a base of knowledge before the issues can be precisely stated.

Although it is natural to set God and chance in opposition we must not fall into the trap of personifying chance as though it could be viewed as a rival to God as the ultimate cause of all things. The habit is longstanding as Tyche, the Greek goddess of chance, Fortuna her Roman counterpart and Lady Luck bear witness. Even those who would never personify chance in such direct terms find it difficult to avoid slipping into the habit of speaking as though 'chance' causes things to happen. When we say that something is due to chance we are not thereby identifying its cause. To say that anything is caused by chance is, strictly speaking, a contradiction in terms. The chance hypothesis, in any sphere, is no more than an acknowledgment of our failure to find a cause. Tychism is not a rival to theism but is, rather, a state of agnosticism about causes.

Our main theological contention will be that a degree of indeterminancy in nature is essential if human choices are not to be illusory. But this view is not without its difficulties. Can it, for example, avoid placing limits on God, so threatening his omniscience or his omnipotence? And if real chance be introduced to preserve human freedom will not this open the door to Monod's anti-theology and with it the end to any meaningful notion of providence? These are clearly weighty questions in which the philosophical and technical aspects of probability are closely interwoven. The task of answering them is made harder by semantic difficulties and problems of communication across the wide range of specialisms which span the enormous territory over which chance phenomena occur.

Historical perspective

We now re-trace our steps in order to elaborate on some of the scientific developments to which we have alluded. A simple chronological catalogue can be misleading if it suggests that there is uniform growth in understanding. Even in contemporary society pre-scientific modes of thought co-exist with those informed by science. The gap between those today who believe in lucky numbers, horoscopes and superstitions and those who honoured Tyche is probably less than that which separates them from their more scientific neighbours. Equally, modern philosophers can still take seriously the views of Aristotle brought together in his *De Bona Fortuna*.[3] It is only too easy to characterize the thought of an age by the writings of its leading thinkers.

Bearing in mind these cautionary remarks a line of development in the changing world view may be traced somewhat as follows. At a primitive level events are assumed to be in the hands of the gods whose capricious behaviour accounts for the unpredictability of events. In the absence of science this is an entirely reasonable interpretation of experience. Things happen for which no reason is apparent. If they cannot be explained in terms of human agency, what is more natural than to suppose that there must be invisible hands behind the scenes? Since earthquakes and thunderstorms are so much more spectacular than anything early man could produce on his own, it is reasonable to infer that the gods are endowed with more power and influence than ourselves. The best hope of influencing events for the benefit of one's crops or health would thus seem to lie in finding favour with those in control. Offerings and sacrifices would be well worthwhile if they appeared to lead to tangible rewards. Although great significance might be attached to individual events, there seems to have been no inkling that there was anything predictable in the aggregate pattern of repetitive events. There could then be no way of seeing any sign of a purposeful God in the chaotic kaleidoscope of events.

The growing recognition by the Jews in Old Testament times that there was one God was a great step forward. It enabled a more coherent view to develop of purpose and design in history and nature. The Jews did not see Yahweh as a capricious being going about his own affairs but as one with a purpose spelt out with growing clarity by law and prophets. He was faithful and could be relied on. In spite of a shifting emphasis discernable in the teaching of Jesus, to which we shall return, the corollary that God was directly responsible for all that happened became deeply embedded in Christian thought. This outlook harmonized well with the emergent science of the seventeenth century. Indeed it has often been argued that Christianity provided an environment which was conducive to the rise of science.[4] For there can be no real incentive to search for pattern and structure in nature without the prior belief that there is some constancy and order to be found there. Thus it was that Newton and many of his co-fellows of the Royal Society of London could rejoice in the beauty and simplicity of the laws which their researches uncovered and so see them as the expression of the divine will. If their religion tended towards deism and was hospitable to Calvinism, God's place in the scheme of things, at least, was secure. As we now turn to outlining some of the discoveries and insights which undermined this tidy view of nature, it is well to remember that Newton's laws are no less accurate now than they were then. It would thus be a mistake to put so much emphasis on the new role of chance as to forget that, on the large scale, order and predictability remain the characteristic features of the world of everyday experience. Although probability theory traces its origins to the very beginning of the scientific revolution its early exponents were largely concerned with games of chance. Its full impact on science was still some way off. Although Newton wrote extensively on theological matters his outlook left no room for chance. Chance was not a theological problem. It became one later when it began to appear that much of the lawful behaviour of the world had its origin in randomness. The need for a controlling God was then much diminished.

Two developments in physics and biology around the turn of the century began to undermine the 'clockwork' image built up by early science. This was summed up in Laplace's assertion that the future of the universe in every detail could, in principle, be predicted from a complete knowledge of the position and motion of every particle in it.[5] In physics, Heisenberg's famous uncertainty principle placed a fundamental limit on what one could know about the position and momentum on an electron. The quantum theory showed that changes of state within the atom occurred in a totally unpredictable manner. It thus began to appear that there was an irreducible element of chance at the most fundamental level of the material universe. Einstein rebelled against this picture of matter, preferring to believe that the probabilities of the quantum physicists were merely descriptions of ignorance which would no longer be needed when the discovery of some finer structure of matter made all determinate again. On the philosophical side Popper appears to hold a similar view. Einstein's God was a God of order and there was no place in his scheme of things for a God who, in his famous phrase, 'plays dice with the world'.[6] The matter does not seem to have received the attention it deserves in theological circles. Many discussions go little beyond expressing a welcome relief that flexibility and mystery have found their way back into science. A notable exception was W. G. Pollard's book *Chance and Providence*[7] which both set out clearly what was at stake and offered a solution. His contribution will be discussed in Chapter 6.

By contrast, the second development, in biology, attracted much more attention from Christians of all sorts. But, as we have already noted, it was the apparent conflict with belief in literal inspiration of the Bible that gave evolutionary theory such a hostile reception. Its theological implications went much deeper. By suggesting that the varied forms of life had evolved through the chancy matter of natural selection Darwin had questioned the view not only that they had been created like that in a moment of time but also that there was a plan behind their evolution. There were, of course, those who were far-sighted enough to recognize that God's guiding hand might be seen in evolutionary change just as in instantaneous creation but, perhaps, without realizing that there was very little need for such guidance. Even if it might still be necessary to invoke God as prime mover, evolution was self-regulating. Damaging though this was, sufficient mystery remained to provide a refuge for determined believers. Someone, after all, was needed to inject the spark of life at the appropriate juncture in the evolutionary chain or impregnate the foetus with a soul.

It was not until the implication of the work of evolutionary geneticists in the last few decades and, in particular, their discoveries about the genetic code, that the full measure of the threat to religious belief became apparent. It was at this point that Monod dealt his seemingly mortal blow at any idea that there was a 'master-plan' behind the creation. His case was spelt out in detail in his justly famous book *Chance and Necessity*.[8] We shall examine his thesis in some detail in the next chapter but the essence of the argument is that our empirical knowledge of inheritance at the molecular level demonstrates beyond reasonable doubt that evolution does not follow a determinate plan. It proceeds instead by a series of random steps. The actual line of development is only one of an enormous number of possible paths each of which would have given a different world. In summary, there is now, Monod claimed, irrefutable evidence that the genetic mutations on which evolution depends show no evidence whatsoever of design or purpose. On the contrary they are perfectly consistent with a blind and random choice at each juncture.

Strictly speaking, as Monod acknowledged, the new knowledge does not demolish theism. God can still be invoked as the first cause but he has a strictly non-executive role. This means that mankind was an accidental outcome of the universe and to talk of the providence of God is absurd. Monod's book appeared at the beginning of the 1970s and the work on which it is based spans several decades prior to that. The scientific picture has not significantly altered since then though, as we shall see, there have been new developments which make the Christian apologist's task somewhat easier.

Not all scientists, philosophers or theologians would accept Monod's case in its entirety. We may surmise that Einstein would still need to be convinced that there could be no, as yet undiscovered, deterministic mechanism behind the apparent randomness. It is, of course, quite conceivable, as Laplace thought, that our failure to predict some types of event with certainty is simply because we do not have enough information to specify the initial conditions in sufficient detail. Even if such information was available in principle it might well be far beyond the capacity of our brains to comprehend. Many theologians would take a somewhat similar view but whereas the scientist and philosopher might see certainty residing in the iron necessity of a mechanical model or in logic the theologian would see it in the will of God. This is a more flexible view in that it allows the possibility of things being changed by acts of God influenced, perhaps, by the intercession of his people. Monod's fellow-country-man Teilhard de Chardin had a different scientific perspective and reached quite different conclusions.[9] One of the first major reactions to *Chance and Necessity* was a symposium organized by the Teilhard Centre for the Future of Man where scientists and philosophers sympathetic to his outlook sought to evaluate the impact of the new ideas.[10]

As a tail-piece to this section it should be noted that, contrary to what may seem to have been implied by the discussion so far, Monod's view of nature does not necessarily rule out a God capable of acting in the world. An ingenious idea of how this might come about was suggested by Mary Warnock in the symposium mentioned above. She speculated that the whole of creation might, indeed, be the product of chance in just the way that Monod supposed.

> Might it not be that some creative god made a system which could by chance throw up any kind of thing, living or lifeless? It is not necessarily the case that this creative god would be without interest in whatever was in this sense thrown up by the chance of the mutations. If someone wished to provide a theistic answer to the question of how it all started I see no reason why he should not, nor would the god so supposed necessarily be indifferent to the creatures even if, to start off with, there had been no precise plan for them in the creator's mind.[11]

Although I find this 'adoptionist' explanation neither very plausible nor attractive, it shows that, now that human life has appeared, God might be able to interact with such beings to influence the course of events or, even, to act upon the created universe in some way. This alerts us to the fact that the evidence for God's existence and activity might be more easily discerned in the upper reaches of creation than in the lower. Other options will be pursued in Chapter 2.

Chance and accident: social science and history

Chance is also coming to play an increasingly important part in the social sciences, though this has not been widely noticed nor seen as a threat to belief. In the hierarchy of science physics takes pride of place and the view of physicists have carried special weight in the debates on science and religion. After all physics is concerned with the nature of matter at its most fundamental level. Those who incline to a reductionist view of knowledge are inevitably led to physics for the ultimate answers to questions in all branches of science. Nobel prize winners in the physical sciences have therefore been assured of a respectful hearing when they made pronouncements on the religious implications of their researches. Whether they are concerned with the minutest structure of the atom or with the origin of the universe in the 'big bang', they are obviously working at the limits of the human mind. This is how Pollard, himself a physicist as well as priest, seems to have seen it. Now that biologists are increasingly concerned with the mechanism of heredity and the origin of life they too are in a privileged position in relation to the great theological questions of origins and purposes.

There is much force in this line of argument but if we reject the reductionist view and suppose that as more complex organizations of matter are formed so there appear qualitatively new phenomena which cannot be wholly explained in terms of their physics and chemistry, then other considerations apply. The higher forms of matter, including those which are living, display in a richer form the potentialities inherent in creation. Taking up the remark at the end of the last section there are good grounds for expecting the finger of God to be more readily discernible at the higher end of the evolutionary spectrum than at the lower. The logical end of this line of reasoning is that it is on the behaviour of man that the science and religion debate should be primarily focussed. We thus turn to the social sciences and to history to see whether we can rid ourselves of the apparent randomness and purposelessness which be-devils the basic sciences. Here at least we might expect cause and purpose to be more clearly in evidence. It is certainly to history and human experience that theologians have usually appealed for empirical support for belief in a providential God.

Undoubtedly there are radical differences between the natural and social sciences, but there is a surprising amount that is common. Socially interesting quantities vary in much the same unpredictable fashion as their counterparts in biology. For example, the length of time that computer programmers stay in their jobs, the size distributions of firms in a given industry and television viewing patterns all exhibit that regularity in the aggregate combined with individual unpredictability that is characteristic of so many physical processes. The same probability theory that is used to model the one works equally well for the other. Complex social processes like the diffusion of innovations or riot behaviour are analysed in a similar way to chemical reactions. We therefore have to consider whether the randomness we observe here is not equally destructive of traditional belief.

This trend towards the stochastic (i.e. probabilistic) analysis of social phenomena is not a new one. In 1835 Adolphe Quetelet, the Belgian Astronomer Royal published his two volume work *Essai de Physique Sociale*.[12] His *Letters on the Theory of Probabilities as Applied to the Moral and Political Sciences* formed part of the early education of Prince Albert.[13] As the title of the former suggests, Quetelet believed that the regularities observed in social phenomena were amenable to treatment in the same way as those of physics. The difficulties inherent in this somewhat over-optimistic and simplistic view have become more apparent in the last century and a half to the extent that the main point has been almost forgotten. Much of the *Essai* places on record the empirical evidence showing the remarkable constancy of such things as the suicide rates in major cities from year to year. The parallel with physical laws was striking. Although the probability tools at Quetelet's disposal were meagre, he was the pioneer of a field of study which had to await the modern theory of stochastic processes and computing resources to come to fruition. The ever-practical Florence Nightingale, his contemporary and admirer, saw these social 'laws' as tools to be used for the amelioration of social ills. She saw the infant social science giving men power over their social environment and saw the laws demonstrating the order and constancy of God just as their physical counterparts did.[14]

From these modest beginnings stochastic modelling in the social sciences has become an important feature of economics, psychology, sociology, political science and, even history. Not surprisingly, this movement has attracted opposition on the humanistic ground that man cannot be treated as a creature subject to the laws of chance. The idea seems to call into question the dignity of human nature and the reality of rational behaviour. The fallacy in this reaction lies in supposing that, because certain aspects of human behaviour have something in common with those of aggregates of particles or bacteria and suchlike, they must share all features in common. This is as absurd as supposing that, because both man and coal can be weighed, man is no more than a sack of coal. There is however, a more substantial point to be made. When discussing physical events it appeared that if we traced the causal links back to their origin we should eventually reach the random happenings at the heart of the atom. These unco-ordinated and chaotic events did not look like the coherent expression of the will of a purposive God. By contrast, when we do the same exercise with events in the behavioural sphere, the path of causation takes us back to a decision of an individual (or individuals) which was then acted upon. In so far as the exercise of individual free will can be regarded as an explanation there is no mystery. What may mimic randomness when viewed on the large scale appears perfectly explicable at the individual level. Of course, it is possible to maintain that human free will is an illusion and that apparently purposeful behaviour is no more than the product of random firings of neurons in the brain. In that case the road of reductionism would lead us back ultimately to physics and there would be no essential difference between the social and natural sciences. This kind of argument is notorious for implying that the line of reasoning which led us to this conclusion must itself be the product of chance events and hence be totally worthless. The real point to be made is that whether randomness is ascribed to chance, as in the case of the atom, or to free-will, as with ourselves, in neither case is it clear where God fits in. Although we may readily concede that apparently random behaviour does not imply a common explanation it is not easy to see how God can be present in either. Independent and unrelated activity does not seem to bear the imprint of the kind of God that Christians worship. The challenge posed to theology by the social sciences is thus a real one.

There are, of course, many occasions when large aggregates of people do behave in a co-ordinated and purposeful way – war for example. On such occasions the laws of probability may not need to be invoked and this fact certainly weakens the argument which we are mounting. Nevertheless, the existence of much unpredictability, especially in just those circumstances in which people are least subject to constraints, does raise serious questions about providence.

History is made up of the sum of events which social scientists study on a smaller canvas. What we have already said must therefore bear upon the general question of how God acts in history. One of the central ideas of Christian theology down the centuries has been that God is a God who acts in events. This idea comes through strongly in the Old Testament and has been a prominent strand of Christian thinking ever since. Some have seen history as the story of a few great men directing the course of events and moulding others to their will by coercion or persuasion. God's role can then be seen as closely associated with a relatively small number of key individuals. However, a moment's reflection on our own experience of events, great and small, will serve to weaken any credence we may have initially given to this view. Many historians, Herbert Butterfield included, have taken a different view. He said:

It is necessary, however, to remember that the pattern of the history making which we shall carry out will not be the product of my will or yours or indeed of anybody elses, but will represent in one sense rather what might almost seem to be a compounding of these wills or at least of their effects – something which sometimes no single person will either have intended or anticipated. And even so the pattern will be complicated by certain other factors superadded-factors which it is sometimes difficult for the historian either to analyze or to explain.[15]

This picture is not so very far removed from that which we have mentioned as occurring in physical processes. What happens is just the aggregated effect of a very large number of individual decisions and happenings deriving no sense of direction or purpose from any supernatural source. Against this must be set another feature of history which does not come out in the quotation from Butterfield, and this too has its analogue in physical and biological processes. There are apparently insignificant events which have far-reaching consequences in much the same manner as genetic mutations. For example, the great fire of London began as a local conflagration started accidentally and which fanned by a wind, destroyed a large part of the city. Without the initial accident the plan and architecture of London today might have been very different and Sir Christopher Wren's name might never have reached the history books. Again, John Wesley's birth depended on a number of apparently unrelated events – the disagreement of his parents about praying for William III, the latter's subsequent death and the consequential return home of John's father Samuel, and so on. Had any link in this chain been otherwise and had not the young John been subsequently rescued from the burning rectory at Epworth, the social and religious history of England might have been very different. Had Hitler been killed when the attempt was made on his life in July 1944, the later course of the second world war and post-war history would have taken a different course. The fact that he was not killed resulted from the interruption of Stauffenberg so that he could not put as much explosive as he intended into the briefcase that was to be planted under the table in the conference room, and then that someone moved the case because it was in the way. On such 'accidents' hangs the course of history. It may be justly argued that there are many equally important events which have been deliberately planned and executed but the hazards which beset even the best laid schemes serve to emphasize the element of unpredictability in history.

We have moved from the realm of chance in science to accident in history. It is desirable to maintain a distinction between the two terms, and we shall do so later, but for the present it is not important. What is common to both is the lack of predictability and apparent absence of purpose.

We can easily supplement the illustrations of how accidents produce great consequences from our own experience in matters of career, marriage and such like. Joseph Conrad captured the essence of such situations in an author's note to his novel *Chance*. He explains how he set aside the story at one point. On taking it up again the plot could have taken either of two courses. 'My sympathies being equally divided and the two forces being equal it is perfectly obvious that nothing but mere chance influenced my decision in the end. It is a mighty force that of mere chance; absolutely irresistible yet manifesting itself often in delicate forms such for instance as the charm, true or illusory, of a human being.'[16]

One of his characters in the book says:

And if you ask me how, wherefore, for what reason? I will answer you: Why, by chance! By the merest chance, as things do happen, lucky and unlucky, terrible or tender, important or unimportant; and even things which are neither, things so completely neutral in character that you would wonder why they do happen at all if you didn't know that they, too, carry in their insignificance the seeds of further incalculable chances.[17]

James Hilton weaves a similar theme into his novel *Random Harvest*.[18]

The shift from natural science through social science to history provides no escape from the challenge of chance. In the case of history it is, perhaps, easier to argue that what seems to us the merest chance is actually the deliberate act of a purposeful God. And since it is impossible to show that such a view is logically incoherent it must be reckoned as a possible explanation. But, by the same token, we must allow that things may actually be just what they seem to be, that is accidental, and then there is a case to answer. In making a choice between these options we must be chary of leaning too heavily on the claim that a providential explanation is logically compatible with the scientific world view if in doing so we have to indulge in special pleading of a highly implausible kind. Ideally we would like to show that the world of chance and accident is not merely compatible with our theology but is actually required by it.

Aims and outline

Although chance raises serious theological questions across the whole spectrum of knowledge it has received most attention in the biological and physical sciences where the issues are relatively well-defined. We shall therefore concentrate initially on this area, focussing particularly on evolutionary biology where the question has been so clearly put by Monod. His case is considered in Chapter 2 along with some of the replies, Christian and otherwise. A full evaluation of the position must await the discussion of chance and certainty which comes later. The perspective of Chapter 3 is quite different in that it examines the validity of arguments which purport to use the apparent randomness in nature to establish, rather than demolish, theism. On one side we have those who assert that because chance is the rule in heredity there can be no master-plan; on the other are those who claim that what has actually occurred is so improbable on the chance hypothesis that it must be abandoned. We shall aim to test the strength of both positions.

The core of the book is in Chapters 4 and 5 which mark the transition from the scientific perspective to one which is primarily theological. Rather than accepting the common view that chance is inimicable to order and purpose, we shall aim to show that it is actually conducive to the kind of world which one would expect a God such as Christians believe in to create. Instead of opposing God and chance, we shall contend that chance was God's idea and that he uses it to ensure the variety, resilience and freedom necessary to achieve his purposes. This, of course, raises serious theological problems and the remaining two chapters contain a first attempt to work out some of the implications. Above all these are concerned with God's ability to control, or influence, events in the world.

In a book which attempts to span such a broad range of disciplines some remarks are in order about the author's pre-suppositions. On the scientific side there is little to be said. I adopt the 'commonsense' view of scientific activity as an attempt to describe and understand an objective world 'out there'. It is common nowadays to emphasize that we impose a subjective structure on our observations – our facts are theory-laden. This is obviously true, but it is easy to let the recognition of this truth obscure the objective content of science. I believe that the structure of the world is adequately, though incompletely, described by those scientific theories and models which have stood the test of experiment.

A theological stance is much more difficult to specify. One can regard either science or theology as definitive so that the exercise of reconciling the two consists of accepting in one what is consistent with the other and rejecting the rest. It is difficult to persist in this line without doing violence to truth or one's integrity. The alternative is to take the commendable line of trying to give equal weight to both, but this is liable to end in a compromise which does justice to neither. The situation is not unlike that obtaining in biblical studies in the early days of higher criticism. Many faced the dilemma of whether to follow the new critical methods wherever they led or whether to hold fast to the theory of literal inspiration in which they had been raised. A. S. Peake, who did so much to show that critical studies could go hand-in-hand with a deep and intellectually satisfying faith said:

> It is, of course, true that all unprejudiced investigation has its risks. It is conceivable that its results may be fatal to faith. We cannot accept the well-meant but cowardly advice that we should decline to imperil our faith by scrutiny of the grounds on which it rests.[19]

This statement can be applied with equal force in the present context and is one with which I heartily concur. In this sense I give priority to science in the matter of establishing the way that things are in the world. There are risks in subjecting belief to scrutiny in the light of scientific knowledge. There is a risk in faith itself and we shall later come close to the view that God himself takes (and has taken) real risks. Risk seems to be deeply embedded in the very nature of things. Christian history shows that those who have been prepared to take risks have often been rewarded by a fuller and deeper understanding of God's nature and purpose.

Scientific enquiry demands a degree of agnosticism and there can thus be little fruitful dialogue with those whose position rests on a rigid fundamentalism derived from biblical literalism. There is, however, a conservative position in both matters from which one can engage in serious debate about the place of chance in science and religion. Though I have much sympathy with this latter approach, I think that it ultimately leads to a less majestic view of creation than is to be had by a less dogmatic and more open approach to what God is saying in nature. But this must be combined with an equal recognition that God also speaks in other ways. What he says in the Bible is illuminated rather than contradicted by science.

2

Chance and Necessity

The devastating attack on belief in a purposeful God made by Jacques
Monod, in his *Chance and Necessity*[1] is the most penetrating and
damaging that has been launched in the name of science. To quote his
own words in a BBC interview with Sir Peter Medawar when the
English translation of the book appeared, we now have 'biological
proof of the absence of a master-plan' and 'belief in a universe in
which man was destined to appear is contrary to modern biology'.[2]
One of the time-honoured counters to the atheist who points to the
lack of proofs of God's existence is to reply that disproofs are equally
hard to come by. Monod claimed to have changed all that by showing
how modern biology now provides just such proof. We noted this
claim in Chapter 1 and must now examine the evidence more closely.

To avoid possible misunderstanding, it should be said at once that
Monod's proof does not concern the existence of a creator at the
beginning of time to start the whole process off. He claims, rather to
show that, even if there were such a God, he could have had no
subsequent control over the way that his creation developed. For all
practical (religious) purposes, therefore, he might just as well not
exist. If true, then Monod's claim would be sufficient to demolish
Christianity and most of the other higher religions. In view of this it is
surprising that the claim by a highly reputable scientist should not
have stimulated more interest among theologians. Philosophers and
scientists with theological interests have rallied to the defence of
orthodoxy and to the criticism of Monod's science and philosophy.
We shall examine some of these responses in detail and, for the most
part, find them wanting. One would have thought that the seriousness
of the challenge was at least equal to that of biological doubts about the
virgin birth, yet it has produced nothing like the turmoil in theological
circles.

We begin by reviewing Monod's case in sufficient detail for the force of his conclusions to become apparent. Then we consider responses from theologians, scientists and philosophers to these claims with a view to seeing what, if anything can be salvaged. Our conclusion will be that more remains than Monod would have us believe, but that the positions taken up by many of the critics are far from satisfactory. However, there are hints at a solution which we shall explore and develop later in the book.

Monod's case

In his book, Monod describes the macro molecular processes by which organisms replicate themselves and explains how natural selection operating on purely random variations leads to the evolution of all living things. It is the fact that the nature of the changes, known as mutations, are quite unrelated to the viability of the resulting change in the organism which leads to the denial of any possibility of a directing purpose. So that there shall be no mistaking the clear and categorical terms in which this assertion is made let Monod speak for himself. Speaking of mutations he says:

> We say that these events are accidental, due to chance. And since they constitute the *only* possible source of modifications in the genetic text, itself the *sole* repository of the organism's hereditary structures, it necessarily follows that chance *alone* is at the source of every innovation, of all creation in the biosphere. Pure chance, absolutely free but blind, at the very root of the stupendous edifice of evolution: this central concept of modern biology is no longer one among other possible or even conceivable hypotheses. It is today the *sole* conceivable hypothesis, the only one compatible with observed and tested fact. And nothing warrants the supposition (or the hope) that conceptions about this should, or ever could, be revised.[3]

This is as clear and uncompromising a statement as one is ever likely to come across on such a vital matter. Monod's own italics underline the sharpness of the knife which he is taking to the roots of traditional belief. There is, of course, the question of what precisely is meant by 'due to chance' and this will have to be critically examined later. First we summarize some of the scientific background on which these assertions are based.

It is not necessary to go fully into the details of the processes by which cells reproduce themselves. This is beautifully expounded for the layman by Monod himself in *Chance and Necessity*, it provides the theme of Watson's *Double Helix*[4] and was the subject of the annual

Christmas lectures to young people at the Royal Institution in London in 1980. It is a fascinating story, but it is sufficient here to give the bare bones so as to isolate the role played by chance and thus gauge the strength of Monod's case.

At the centre of things is DNA (deoxyribonucleic acid) which for our purposes may be thought of as a string of four distinguishable elements denoted by A, G, C and T; these are the letters of the genetic alphabet. DNA is involved in the manufacture of proteins which are composed of amino acid residues. The particular sequence of elements in the DNA determines what protein will be produced. It takes a group of three DNA elements to specify each amino acid residue. The genetic code is a table linking each possible DNA triplet to its associated residue. The DNA molecules actually come in pairs. Each element in one chain (A, G, C or T) is linked with its complement in the second chain (A to T, C to G). Replication of the molecule takes place by the two chains separating. A new partner for each of the elements in the separated chains is then found by complementary pairing so that, in the end, the original double strand is replaced by two identical double strands. The new molecules can then go about the production of a cell identical with the parent.

If this were the whole story, the future development of living things would be strictly determined. However, this does not happen because another factor enters the picture. Accidents may occur in the process of replication which change the DNA sequence in the offspring. For example, chemical agents may temporarily alter the pairwise affinities so that A becomes linked to C. Elements can be accidentally deleted or added and ionizing radiations can also cause changes. Such changes are called mutations. When they occur, proteins manufactured by the offspring DNA will be different and the organisms of which they form part will have different properties. Such mutations introduce *variability* into replication and variation is the raw material on which natural selection works. Some changes will be deleterious to the organism whereas others will be neutral or confer an advantage. Those organisms which benefit in this way will prosper and ensure that the new arrival persists and becomes established. Any living thing, a man or a worm, therefore stands at the end of a long succession of such changes and what he or it is, is ultimately the product of random mutations in evolutionary history. According to Monod these mutations are entirely unpredictable and, hence, what has happened is only one of an enormous number of possible courses which evolution could have taken. The randomness actually enters into the argument in two ways which make a purposive interpretation difficult to maintain. The first arises from the arbitrariness of the genetic code. In essence this means that the biological consequences of a particular mutation are entirely unpredictable from the change in the DNA. If 'purpose' were at work one would expect to find a relationship between changes in the DNA and the properties of the associated protein. Putting it crudely, if the levers of change are in the DNA sequence then someone who pulls a lever would be able to predict what result would follow. Monod asserts that there is overwhelming empirical evidence that there is no such relationship. The second random feature concerns the event of mutation itself – where and when it occurs. This is also unpredictable because it is a consequence of a microscopic quantum event depending on the essential uncertainty present at that level.

The nature of Monod's proof should now be clear. If the world was the outworking of a divine purpose according to a masterplan, one would expect to find some evidence for this at the key points where change occurs. That is, mutations, in timing and effect, would be related to some discernible purpose for the organism in the mind of the Creator. In short, there would be a reason for everything that happened. This is not what we find. Mutations are entirely consistent with the hypothesis that all change is by accident. The expected linkage between action and outcome which is the characteristic of purposive action is entirely lacking. Furthermore the would-be theist has a double obstacle to overcome. Even if – as Einstein was disposed to believe – the inherent uncertainty at the quantum level could be shown to be explicable in deterministic terms, the independence of the kind of mutation and the properties of the protein would remain.

There seem to be two ways out of the difficulty for the Christian apologist. Either Monod's science is wrong or his theological deductions from it are at fault. On the scientific front the essentials of Monod's case have not been seriously challenged, though it is claimed to be incomplete at a number of points. For example, Waddington[5] and others have pointed out that fitness for survival is not usually dependent on a single gene but on the whole genetic make-up of the organism. A gene which is disadvantageous in some combinations may be neutral or even advantageous in other combinations or in other environments. Although a great many variations may be thrown up by mutation, the process of selection is not at all random. R. E. Monro in *Beyond Chance and Necessity* examines the adequacy of Monod's science.[6] He emphasizes the enormous areas of ignorance in this field contrasted with the small amount of knowledge and argues that there might be a revolution in biological thinking which would throw our present understanding into the melting pot. Waddington, contrary to Monod, claims that gene mutation is not random in a complete sense and that the chemical processes involved can be studied and eventually understood in strictly causal terms. But he points out that this would not affect the vital point that such changes are not causally connected with the natural selective forces which will determine its success or failure in producing offspring in the next generation. Monod's deduction that the essential randomness of the process could not have been predicted at the outset is open to serious doubt, as we shall see. But that does not call into question the basic correctness of his science. At present, therefore, there appears to be no escape for the theologian along this path. There might be some minor accommodation, but Monro's revolution has not yet occurred.

Before going on to see what other defence can be made, we note another role that chance plays in evolution which makes the apologist's task more difficult. In a *New Scientist* article entitled 'The Chance that Shapes Our End' Stephen Jay Gould argued that random processes do more than provide the basic variability on which natural selection works.[7] These new sources of uncertainty operate independently of those which we considered so far.

The first aims to explain how new species can arise by random genetic processes which have nothing to do with fitness for survival. It stems from the idea of a neutral mutation, that is, one which confers neither advantage nor disadvantage. Evolution by natural selection is usually based on the supposition that most mutations will be deleterious and hence will quickly die out because their bearers will not survive to reproduce. A few mutations will confer an advantage and those who possess them will eventually oust their competitors by their greater fitness for survival. Gould claims that some mutations fall into neither category and, hence, that they will spread within a population in a random fashion, their survival and dispersion not depending on the qualities they confer. Which ones survive in these circumstances is thus a matter of chance. If we have 'harem' type breeding in which one male mates with many females and where brother/sister mating occurs, it is possible for pure mutants to arise and propagate. Those species which arise by this means would not be fashioned by the environment but by means entirely unrelated to it. In this sense, therefore, they at least could not have been planned.

The second way in which Gould sees chance shaping our ends is through accidental disasters which wipe out whole species unselectively. He quotes calculations, for example, that in the major catastrophe at the end of the Permian period about 225 million years ago as many as 96% of all species then existing may have been wiped out. (This calculation is based on data for sea-urchins but the same kind of reasoning would, Gould claims, hold generally.) Throughout geological history there appear to have been at least five major extinctions in the biological world. McLaren (whose dating differs slightly from Gould) discusses the evidence that these disasters may have been caused by impact with the earth of large meteorites.[8] The matter is obviously complicated, but he concludes that two of these have a sufficiently high probability of being caused by impacts to be taken seriously. One of these coincides with the extinction of the dinosaurs. Other causes of major extinctions include solar and orbital changes and convection in the mantle of the earth, producing changes in the sea level and the climate.

In such wholesale destruction it is hardly conceivable that the few per cent of survivors would have been providentially protected to ensure the success of a divine plan. If God were really in charge, it would be more natural to have expected him to avoid the disasters altogether rather than tailor them to safeguard the long-term future. Once again the introduction of cosmic 'accidents' cries out for an examination of what is really meant by an accident in this context and how it relates to other occurrences of 'chance' in the scheme of things.

Some replies

Before looking at the very varied responses to Monod's thesis (and by implication Gould's extension of it) it may help to focus our thinking by outlining two extreme reactions which are possible within a theistic framework.

The first, recognized by Monod in his broadcast conversation with Medawar, is that the argument is not a strict proof: 'a religious plan can never be disputed, of course'. It is entirely coherent to maintain, in the face of the scientific evidence, that every detail of the universe's evolution conforms to a pre-determined masterplan. As we shall see, this has been argued on both scientific and theological grounds. From the theological viewpoint it requires God to have created things in such a way that his presence and purpose is entirely concealed from scientific investigation. It is almost as though the world was designed to have the appearance of an accident so that it would lead intelligent beings, like Monod, who look no further than the created world, to rationally conclude that it expressed no purpose. The theological objection to this view is that it reflects adversely on the character of God. It puts one on a par with those fundamentalist Christians who are alleged to believe that God placed fossils in the rocks to confound presumptuous scientists. A God who deliberately sets out to mislead or deceive us is scarcely compatible with one who gave us minds to use for his glory.

At the other extreme, it is possible to accept the whole of Monod's argument and still maintain that a world of beings such as ourselves was part of the divine plan. According to this view, we are compelled to allow that the occurrence of life on this planet in this part of the universe is extremely remote. However, the probability is clearly not zero otherwise we should not be here to ask the question! That being so it is clearly possible for a God of unlimited power and resources to create a universe so large (or so many universes) that the chance of achieving his object becomes as near certain as he chooses to make it. Just as the proverbial monkey, typing at random, will eventually produce Shakespeare's plays, so a God who tries often enough will, sooner or later, produce beings such as ourselves. The time, space and matter required would be so enormous as to defy comprehension and strain credibility to the limit, but there is nothing logically impossible about it. According to this view God is not seen as controlling events in any sense, at least up to the point at which sentient beings appear. There is then no difficulty in admitting a role for providence at the level of mind as long as it does not interfere with the essential randomness of sub-atomic and biological processes. The theological difficulties which this approach poses are many and various but, again, one chiefly recoils at its implications for the character of a God who chooses(?) to operate in this way. While it certainly exalts the power of God, it is power of the 'brute force and ignorance' variety, entirely lacking in the finer qualities of planning and control. In short it magnifies power at the expense of intelligence. It puts God on a par with the baboon in the limerick;

> There was once a hairy baboon,
> Who always breathed down a bassoon,
> For he said it appears
> In billions of years
> I shall certainly hit on a tune.

It would, of course, still be possible to maintain that the personal attributes of the god, such as love and justice, were not inconsistent with this view. Nevertheless, one is entitled to expect a more natural and elegant account of God's role which does not have to graft the higher attributes on to such an ungainly frame as this interpretation of science thrusts upon us.

One of the first co-ordinated responses to Monod's thesis was the symposium, already mentioned, edited by John Lewis entitled *Beyond Chance and Necessity: A critical enquiry into Professor Jacques Monod's Chance and Necessity*.[9] Published by the Garnstone Press in 1974 in the Teilhard Study Library this brought together the views of philosophers and scientists, many of them, but not all, sympathetic to Teilhard de Chardin's comprehensive view of the whole creation moving along its destined path towards its culmination in the omega point. Monod's view stands in stark contrast to this philosophy and one might expect the clash of outlooks to highlight the essential issues. Not all of the contributions deal directly with the role of chance, but most of those that do are covered in what follows. Of the many books and articles which have engaged in the debate since, *Anti-Chance* by E. Schoffeneils describes itself as a reply to Monod's *Chance and Necessity* and bases its case on scientific grounds – it is anti-theistic as well as anti-chance.[10] From a conservative Christian standpoint Donald M. MacKay's 1977 Riddell Memorial Lectures entitled *Science, Chance and Providence*, though not specifically a reply to Monod, range broadly but briefly over the whole field.[11] More recently, A. R. Peacocke's 1978 Bampton Lectures, published as *Creation and the World of Science*, expounds a view in which chance is given a more positive place in the purposes of providence.[12] It is convenient to deal with these and other responses according to the viewpoint which they adopt. These are summarized, somewhat inadequately, by the following section headings.

A conservative Christian view

We begin with a view which stands close to the first of the two extremes which we mentioned at the outset. It has been clearly expressed by MacKay both in the Riddell lectures and in his book *The Clockwork Image*.[13] In the former he has a chapter called 'The mythology of chance' in which he addresses himself to Monod's claims. According to MacKay, Monod has made a simple error. He has confused the scientific and mythological uses of the word chance. This means, in effect, that he has personified chance by regarding it as an explanation for what has occurred. This implies the assumption that there are two possible explanations for the world – God or chance – and that we must opt for one or the other. If, as Monod claims, a complete and satisfactory explanation can be given in terms of chance, then the 'God hypothesis' is ruled out. MacKay rejects this dichotomy denying that chance can be set up as an alternative to God. 'Chance in science', he writes, 'is not the name of a thing or an agent, least of all a *cause* or a *source* of anything; it stands for the *absence* of an assignable cause.'[14] To MacKay, the existence of events for which no assignable cause can be found is no argument against God. God is sovereign and free and he can therefore choose to do things, some of which may be seen as consequences of antecedent events, while others are entirely unpredictable, humanly speaking. In particular, the fact that mutations and such like appear to us to be completely random does not mean that they are not caused (and planned) by God. There is nothing in the Bible to say that every event must have an assignable cause. In short, chance does not rule out God, chance is simply a description of one way of God's acting. Modern biology therefore has nothing to say against theism since there is nothing in it which is incompatible with the idea of an all powerful and purposeful God.

In logic MacKay's case cannot be faulted. Since things have actually turned out as they have there is no inconsistency in maintaining that this outcome coincides exactly with what a purposeful God intended. Although staggering to the human mind, God must be seen as in detailed control of the movement of every elementary particle everywhere in the universe from the beginning of time, until now and for ever. The things that appear random to us in our ignorance are part of a vast plan in the mind of God in which every minutest detail has been (or is being) worked out by God. As we noted, Monod allows that this account is an option – he simply regards is as incredible. For MacKay such a belief is rooted in the sovereignty of God. If it were to be true that anything, no matter how insignificant, took place without his knowledge or intent, his sovereignty would be impugned. The quotation from Proverbs 16.33 that 'The lots may be cast into the lap, but the issue depends wholly on the Lord' is the cornerstone of his approach. In essence, therefore, MacKay resolves the God or chance dilemma by abolishing chance. Chance enters our descriptions merely as a way of accommodating our ignorance. If we could see things as God sees them, all would be explained with no uncertainty at all.

There is much in MacKay's argument to be applauded. His clear rejection of the God versus chance dichotomy can be wholeheartedly accepted. All causal chains if traced far enough back must reach a point at which explanations fail. For the theist, this is the natural point to invoke God's direct action. A 'chance' event marks just such a point. As an event with no antecedent cause that can be identified the only possibility remaining is to attribute it to the action of a free, purposive Being. Taken together with the belief, derived from other and independent sources, in the existence of a beneficient and almighty heavenly Father, Monod's arguments pose no threat. Indeed, we could argue further that without uncertainty there would be more reason to doubt, since in a fully predictable world God's freedom to act as he willed might seem limited.

In spite of its logical force and sound biblical foundation I find MacKay's explanation unsatisfactory. To my mind it sidesteps the full force of Monod's case by maintaining that the logical possibility of the explanation offered is sufficient to establish its credibility. There are a great many explanations of a multitude of happenings which though possible are not in the least likely. It is logically possible, as Bertrand Russell said, that the whole of creation together with our memories of the past could all have been created five minutes ago, or that no one exists but ourselves. Yet hardly anyone seriously believes such things. Although the whole of nature could have come about as the execution of a highly detailed master plan, there is, in fact, nothing to distinguish it (at the micro-biological level) from one in which Monod, at least, could see no plan at all. Monod might justly say that if a purposive God was really at work one might expect his mode of operation to be clearly distinguishable from the actions of one who simply 'plays dice'. The onus is on MacKay to explain why, if God is really in charge, he behaves in such an apparently capricious manner. To reply that 'God moves in a mysterious way' and that we cannot expect to understand all the whys and wherefores does not explain why, even in the limited area which we can understand, the signs are so ambiguous. Perhaps the abolition of chance was premature and unnecessary. On MacKay's own argument chance is not a thing or agent and so allowing it back does not represent a challenge to the sovereignty of God. Rather it challenges us to discover how there can be a place for it in the divine economy.

A conservative scientific view

A direct refutation of Monod's doctrine has been made by the Belgian biochemist E. Schoffeniels.[15] His book *Anti-Chance* is described on the cover as a reply to Monod. As its title suggests it confronts him head on by denying that chance plays any part in the evolution and development of life. The sense in which the book is a reply is not clear. Schoffeniels' distaste for attributing anything to chance is made abundantly clear, but there is surprisingly little reference to *Chance and Necessity*, and hardly any attempt to engage in serious argument on the main issue. In fact much of the book is taken up with an account of the author's biochemical interests interspersed with chapters on such things as probability, information theory and cybernetics. In spite of the obscurity and lack of direction of much of the argument the conclusion reached on the last page is clear enough:

> Whether we recognize it or not, we are here because about three million years ago conditions on earth and the properties of the elements were such as to ensure it. To certain minds, it is as despairing to be the fruit of necessity as it is that of chance. No matter how aesthetically moving, the pathetic efforts of all the

religions and most of the philosophies in blindly denying the reality of the human condition against all the evidence produce only chaos and heroic but absurd somersaults. Obscurantism has had its day. Let there be light![16]

This passage conveys not only the author's conclusion, but also the flavour of the more polemical passages. It also makes clear that Schoffeniels does not oppose chance on behalf of God or religion. He does not discuss the question of how or why conditions came to be as they were about three million years ago or, for that matter, how the universe began. He advocates a strict scientific determinism at the macro level. It is admitted that apparent randomness exists at the sub-atomic level but at the molecular level, which is what matters for his purposes, all is determined. There are no molecular events, he claims, which do not have a cause in antecedent events and therefore no events which, in principle, cannot be foreseen. This is not to imply that all things are working to a pre-determined end, but rather to that end which is implicit in the original state; it is a determinism without purpose. It is not clear whether Schoffeniels' determinism extends to the higher levels of consciousness and thus, whether his own views and those of Monod are to be seen as no more than the inevitable consequences of the state of the world three million years ago.

If Schoffeniels is right and Monod wrong, then one ought to be able to obtain relevant experimental evidence to decide between them. Monod lays great store by the principles of objectivity according to which, truth is that which can be established on a firm empirical base. Schoffeniels does, in fact, quote some experimental evidence from the work of Fox and Wachneldt which he claims does contradict the Monod doctrine. The experiment in question involved heating a mixture of amino acids in which the various acids were present in equal amounts. The heating synthesizes polypeptide chains. If Monod is right, then Schoffeniels claims that the various possible combinations ought to occur in equal amounts. However, according to Fox and Wachneldt, some polypeptides appear much more frequently than others. Hence it cannot be true that all the possible combinations are equally likely. Whether or not Monod does claim that all combinations must be equally likely, I am not competent to judge, but the conclusion that Schoffeniels draws from the data is certainly wrong. He says 'This observation contradicts another dogma of molecular biology according to which the sequence of amino acids of a polypeptide is due to chance'.[17] It does nothing of the kind. It shows that the chances are not *equal* but it does not mean that the outcome is entirely predictable. If a coin has a probability of 9/10 of falling tails, the outcome of a single toss is, in a sense, less unpredictable than if the chance had been a half but it is unpredictable all the same. To show that the chances of amino acids forming all possible combinations are not equal, reduces the uncertainty but it does not eliminate it.

Perhaps the most telling point made by Schoffeniels is in relation to some work of Prigogine and his colleagues, also working in Belgium but in Brussels.[18] This concerns what are called dissipative structures arising in the study of chemical reactions. A dissipative structure is a stable structure a long way from thermo-dynamic equilibrium which is produced by the amplification of apparently random fluctuations and maintained by a flow of energy. Such discoveries do have important implications for the interpretation of the facts on which Monod bases his case, but Schoffeniels simply challenges the alleged randomness of the fluctuations. He says:

> It is then tempting to consider that the fluctuations represent the random aspect of the phenomenon and that they will correspond to the concept of chance so dear to Jacques Monod.
>
> But because these fluctuations are reproducible, because in a given system they are associated with the production of the same instabilities, is it still permissible to qualify the phenomenon as random?[19]

The reference to instabilities is to states of the system in which the reaction can take one of several future lines of development. Poised as it were at the junction, the merest chance can move it in one direction or another. Once the choice has been made the path is set. It is not clear in what sense the *fluctuations* are repeatable. A repetition of the experiment will certainly involve a system with the same instabilities, but this does not seem to imply the same outcome. The meaning of the claim is somewhat elusive, but if it is intended to mean that chance cannot be operating if the same set-up always leads to the same end then it is false. The rise in pressure of a gas at constant temperature when its volume is halved is a reproducible event, but that is no denial of the random motion of the gas molecules. Similarly there are processes, such as epidemics, which involve a large random element and yet where the final outcome is either certain or highly constrained. The extent to which random processes can be 'used' to achieve desired ends is a central theme of this book and we shall expand on the matter in due course. If I understand him correctly, Schoffeniels is raising a serious point even if it is put in a contentious manner. If it should turn out that the processes by which life arises and develops do, in fact, have predictable outcomes, even though the path to these ends involves genuine randomness, are we justified in attributing the end to chance? If the end is certain but the path by which that end is reached is uncertain, are we any longer justified in following Monod to his anti-providential conclusion? Might not Monod have been so preoccupied with the details of the particular path chosen that he was unable to see the global effects of the process? We are still a long way from such a conclusion but at least we can see how a process might be legitimately described as random and deterministic at the same time!

In his penultimate chapter on *The Structure of Chance* one might have expected Schoffeniels to come to the heart of the matter and set out a definitive alternative to the views of Monod. The alternative presented is based on the flow of information through the system leading to a hierarchy of increasingly complex and organized states. To the layman at least it is not clear how chance is eliminated. The chapter begins with an account of information theory (of the Shannon variety) written with the help of a colleague. The relevance of this is not entirely clear as information and probability are intimately linked. The work of Prigogine and Eigen,[20] which treats evolutionary processes as random, is described with apparent approval yet without it being obvious how the accounts of these authors can be freed from the central role which chance plays in their work. We seem to be thrown back on the fundamental postulate of the author that there is no such thing as chance and, therefore, that there must be some other explanation for the fluctuations which determine the path of the system.

We have dwelt at some length on Schoffeniels' book in spite of the confusing and incomplete nature of its arguments and of its failure to engage in any kind of dialogue with Monod's claims. This is because it touches upon (or stumbles across) several questions which we shall have reason to discuss at greater length later. It also sheds an interesting light upon MacKay's arguments. Although they stand at opposite poles of the theism/atheism spectrum they both opt for an essentially deterministic way out of the problem which chance poses. In Schoffeniels' philosophy man is trapped in a vast machine (of which he is presumably himself a part) which grinds on to some unknown and unplanned destiny. This destiny is implicit in the unknown and unexplained origin of the universe. According to MacKay the course of nature and history is also determined by decisions of God and nothing can happen which is not willed by him. If one knows something of the character of that God and, in particular, that he desires the good of his creatures then MacKay's world is undoubtedly the more attractive to live in. The weakness of both is that it is very difficult to believe in them and, at the same time, give full weight to the empirical evidence of biology.

Philosophical objections

It is to philosophers that we must turn for the most trenchant criticism of Monod's ideas. One of the first of these was Hugo Meynell writing in *The Month* in 1973,[21] and this was quickly followed by the philosophical contributions to the Lewis Symposium published in 1974. Philosophers have the advantage of being able to deploy their professional expertise in an area where Monod was admittedly an amateur. Most are content to leave the science on one side and tackle the short-comings in epistemology. Not all of this by any means concerns the interpretation of chance, so we shall give a partial account suitable for our present purpose.

Meynell's particular target is Monod's adherence to the 'principle of objectivity'. This expresses Monod's claim that nature is objective, that the systematic confrontation of logic and experience is the sole source of true knowledge. In other words, the only true knowledge is that which comes by the application of logical thinking to the data derived from the experience of our senses. Meynell claims that this is to adopt an impossible position. Where does the principle itself come from? Certainly not from science itself; it has to be introduced from outside. One cannot eliminate subjectivity from scientific research. Scientific theories determine the questions that are asked of nature and these are constructs of the human mind. It is at least debatable whether they correspond to anything in the real world. The mere fact that you can ask questions about the universe and obtain empirical answers implies something about its nature. As Meynell puts it, 'the world is either intelligible or it is not; if it is not, then science is impossible; if it is, then "the covenant" which Monod rejects seems to persist in at least one form, and there is at least a good case to be argued for theism'.[22] The 'covenant' referred to here is the alleged harmony between the ways of nature and human thinking which Monod claims must be rejected. Even if we accept this line of argument its conclusion is too weak for our purposes. To argue that, since the world is intelligible, there is a good case to be made for an intelligent Creator takes us no farther than the origin of the world. It does not meet the real force of Monod's case that, whatever the origins, the development of the universe since its beginning shows no signs of a directing purpose. In any event the assertion that no truth can be wholly objective because of the inevitable subjective element in its acquisition may be acceptable as a philosophical proposition. To the working scientist, however, it is not likely to cut a great deal of ice. Being immersed in scientific activity, he is likely to have a powerful sense of the 'rightness' of the pattern which the data reveal – as Monod evidently had. The beauty and coherence displayed as the pieces of the jig-saw come together has a compelling appeal which seems self-authenticating. The fact that this experience can be shared with others gives it a more universal character which, whatever the logical objections, seems to justify its description as objective truth.

Thus far Meynell's argument makes no specific reference to the key role of chance. He turns to this at the end of his article and makes the telling point that Christianity has no brief for determinism. He notes that Monod seems to think that the existence of 'pure, blind' chance counts against theism. On the contrary a deterministic world would leave no room for human freedom and would undermine the whole Christian edifice. A degree, at least, of genuine uncertainty in the scheme of things seems to be essential if human beings are to be anything more than puppets. However, there are problems about going on to say, as Meynell does, 'Monod's arguments about the role of chance events in the origin and evolution of life do not begin to show a lack of design in the universe; they only go to show that, if there is any design, it is not deterministic'.[23] At first sight this sounds like a contradiction. If chance means lack of design or purpose, how can one have a chance design? Design does appear to imply at least some degree of determinism. To say that God designed the world to appear as if it were not designed may be logically innocuous but is somewhat lacking in plausibility. Nevertheless, Meynell's statement can, I believe, be given an interpretation which comes near to the heart of the matter. Suppose we say 'the role of chance events in the origin and evolution of life does not argue against design it rather shows that the universe was designed in such a way that chance had a role to play'. Even if this statement comes perilously close to being a tautology I believe it provides the essential clue to the way out of the corner in which *Chance and Necessity* has placed us.

A second charge which has been made against Monod by philosophers is that he is guilty of reductionism. This theme is particularly prominent in *Beyond Chance and Necessity* and especially in the contribution of the editor John Lewis.[24] Reductionism here means the belief that the complete explanation of any phenomenon is to be found by analysing it into its most elementary components. Thus, all biology can be reduced to chemistry which, in turn, can be reduced to physics. In other words, there is no more to life than what is implied by the behaviour of the elementary particles which make up the living being. This is sometimes characterized as 'nothing-buttery', and as such has been roundly condemned by MacKay[25] and others. The counter claim of the anti-reductionists is that, even in principle, living things cannot be fully explained in terms of the basic sciences. As life evolves and reaches new levels of complexity so it exhibits new features which have no antecedents at the lower levels. Consciousness, for example, is a property of the highly structured brain and nervous system of animals and man which cannot be wholly explained by looking at what preceded it. Since man is now able to influence the direction of evolution, the present and future development of the world is not entirely at the mercy of the purposelessness evident at the lower levels of creation. Room is thus created for the involvement of a purposeful God operating in those higher reaches of the biosphere which have their own autonomy.

I find this a convincing argument, but it contains a serious gap which is almost fatal to the case that the world was planned and is sustained by God. There was a time, presumably, before the emergence of life when these higher levels did not exist, when evolution was an undirected and haphazard business. If, at this stage, the appearance of life was highly improbable we are back to Mary Warnock's hypothesis that God did not (could not?) deliberately plan a universe with life in it but that when, by chance, it happened to occur he capitalized on the fact by becoming involved in the direction of affairs from then on.

Liberal Christian views

We use this description for the views of those who accept the essentials of Monod's scientific case but who attempt to reconcile it with Christian belief. This point of view is represented here by Mary Hesse's[26] contribution to the Anglican symposium *Man and Nature* and by the writings of A. R. Peacocke and especially as they are expressed in his Bampton Lectures of 1978.[27] To some extent they echo the same ideas, but Peacocke in particular introduces important new ingredients into the debate. Since it is in this direction that I believe progress lies it will be necessary to anticipate several themes which will be developed more fully later.

Hesse begins by making the point that Monod's argument concerns the development of nature and not its origin. How was it that matter came into being in the first place with just the right properties to allow the possibility of life? As Paul Davies has more recently pointed out in *The Accidental Universe*,[28] quite minor variations in the initial conditions of the universe would have been fatal to any prospect of life. Evidence of purpose can therefore be found in the rather special combination of circumstances when things began. This is sufficient to retain a place for theism if only of a very limited kind. At best it amounts to a new style deism in which the universe is set going at the beginning of time along an indeterminate path and according to no clear plan. The real thrust of Monod's attack is against the notion that the Creator could have any continuing interest or control.

Hesse's second point is much more penetrating and, at first sight, offers the Christian apologist a firmer base for operations. It had been anticipated by Pollard who made it a central plank of his argument in *Chance and Providence*,[29] and we shall have to examine it again when we come to consider that book in a later chapter. The point is that Monod's theory is statistical and hence does not provide a complete explanation. It says that at any particular juncture any one of a number of outcomes could occur. Each possible outcome would have its own probability of occurring. If that particular situation were to be repeated many times, we could predict that the frequency of each outcome would be in proportion to its probability. But, in fact, there are no repetitions – the situations occur only once. The theory says nothing about how the particular choice is made on that particular occasion. If we are considering a mutation for example, we could imagine listing all the errors in reproduction that could occur. For the sake of argument let us suppose that all these possibilities are equally likely. One of these possibilities is then selected 'by chance'. Here is the gap in the theory where room can be found for God who, it is postulated, actually decides which choice is to be made. Some, at least, of these choices are crucial for the direction which evolution will take. Thus, room is found for God to influence the course of things, and hence one cannot say that the discoveries of science rule out the idea of a purposeful God.

Even if this argument were accepted, it does not require a purposeful God seeking to bring his plans into being. A god who made the decisions by casting lots would be equally compatible with our science or, if such a thing is conceivable, so would some impersonal randomization procedure. But there are other, more cogent, objections. Hesse's proposal could be interpreted in varying ways. If we suppose that God's action is seen in every 'random' event, then we are back to MacKay's position set out earlier and the objections raised when we discussed that apply here also. A weaker version of the argument would be to suppose that God only intervened at a relatively few critical junctures. Thus, if there had been some branch point in evolution such that if one path had been taken the emergence of intelligent life would have been impossible, then God would have acted to keep open the possibility of life. By this means God could have steered the essentially random course of evolution to the point where his involvement at the level of mind became possible. Such a hypothesis is secure from attack on empirical grounds and must therefore be entertained as a serious possibility. Equally, at first sight, it does not appear to reflect adversely on the character of God. Let us, however, look at it more closely. To do this we consider another, much simpler, situation in which chance appears to be at work. This is sex-determination in humans.

In the present state of knowledge we cannot predict whether a given birth will be male or female. Male births occur rather more often than female but to keep the argument as simple as possible let us assume that they are equi-probable. If we have data on a large number of births, we can test the hypothesis that they have occurred independently of one another and with equal probability. Such a sequence of births should have the same statistical characteristics as a sequence of heads and tails in repeated tossings of a coin. Now imagine that in the case of one particular birth it is necessary that it shall be male and that there is outside intervention to ensure that it is so. In a very long sequence of births such a deliberate act would not be detectable. More generally, provided that the proportion of 'special' acts is very small their effects will be swamped by the much larger number of genuinely random effects. To the outside observer a world in which these occasional interferences take place will appear essentially the same as one in which all is of chance. A similar line of reasoning applies in the much more complicated circumstances of evolutionary change. The picture here is of a God who creates a highly complex universe which is largely automatic but needs an occasional minor adjustment to keep it on course. Having reached the stage where intelligent life has become established we then enter a new realm in which chance is not the sole agent in promoting change. Here there is room for the purposive action of God. Hesse also makes the point that the absence of purpose in the lower reaches of evolutionary development would not rule it out in the higher. Human aspirations and will are equally expressive of purpose, and these are outside the biological sphere and they have certainly affected the course of evolution.

Since such an account cannot be refuted on empirical grounds, it must be judged by its internal coherence and, from a Christian point of view, by its harmony with orthodox doctrine. On the former count it is not entirely clear that the very small proportion of interventions which the theory requires would be sufficient to keep evolution on course. It is at least conceivable that a whole sequence of mutations, or whatever, would have to be controlled in detail and that these would represent a departure from the chance laws that would, in principle, be detectable. However, even if we suppose that there are no internal inconsistencies in the theory, it still raises the question of why an all-powerful God should want to work in this way. If he can intervene on some occasions, why not on all? What advantage is there for him in making the minimum of interventions? One answer would be that unpredictability serves other purposes by, for example, creating an environment in which human beings can exercise free choices and so come to full maturity. If this is the case, our effort should be devoted to explaining the reasons why chance may be a tool used by God, and this we shall do in due course. Though this 'minimal intervention theory' may be true, our main reason for casting doubt upon it is that it may be unnecessary. If it turned out that the emergence of mind could be guaranteed without occasional interventions at the molecular level, then intervention would serve no useful purpose.

The most extensive and convincing reply to Monod has come from A. R. Peacocke. Some of the ideas are to be found in his contribution to the symposium *Beyond Chance and Necessity*[30] and his later book *Science and the Christian Experiment*.[31] However, the fullest and latest treatment is in Chapter 3 of his Bampton Lectures published under the title *Creation and the World of Science*.[32] Like MacKay he dismisses the metaphysical notion of chance as something which can be treated as a 'cause' of anything. Like Hesse he points out that the initial conditions of the universe must have been such as to make life possible. He also draws a distinction between two different meanings of 'chance' and points out that much of what we describe in terms of chance may, if fact, be explicable in terms of laws of which we are unaware. To this we shall return. There are, however, new features in Peacocke's treatment which are not found in the writings of the other commentators that we have considered so far.

Peacocke allows a positive role for chance. Implicit in the initial conditions was a vast range of potential universes. Chance allowed all the inherent possibilities to be elicited by 'continually re-shuffling the pack'. This random sorting through of the possibilities is the means by which the potential becomes the actual. He says ' . . . it would be more consistent with the observations to assert that the full gamut of the potentialities of living matter could be explored only through the agency of the rapid and frequent randomization which is possible at the molecular level of the DNA'.[33] Chance mechanisms are thus seen as an efficient means of exploring all the potential forms of matter and thus as being part of the initial design of the universe. This interpretation, I believe, is the clue to a richer and more satisfactory interpretation of chance processes in nature. Peacocke cannot see any reason (and neither can I) why, as Monod supposes, randomness at the molecular level should be seen as evidence of irrationality in the universe. Man is rational and, as we shall see, uses randomness for his own purposes. There is therefore nothing inherently implausible in supposing that in this respect man may be following in the footsteps of his maker. Like most general hypotheses of this kind, it is not immediately clear that it is free of inconsistencies. It requires, for example, that there shall have been enough time since the 'big bang' for sufficient randomization to have taken place to bring about the highly complex living structures which now exist. It also supposes that we can satisfactorily resolve the question as to what chance really is. For example, whether it is possible to talk of purely random events for whose occurrence not even God is directly responsible. If God were directly responsible, then we should be back to MacKay's position in which every event is determined by him. Probabilities then only enter our equations because of our partial ignorance of the true causes.

All of this deals with Monod on his own terms. His science is accepted but, it is claimed, it will not bear the full weight of his philosophical conclusions. Peacocke[34] goes on to describe more recent work by Prigogine and his co-workers in Brussels and by Eigen in Göttingen which calls into question Monod's conclusion that, at the outset, the chance of life appearing in the universe was infinitesimally small. On the contrary it may, as Eigen thinks, have been virtually certain. How it comes about that a process which develops in an unpredictable way should lead to a predictable outcome is something to be investigated in Chapter 4. For the moment we briefly report on the work in question. Prigogine's work is concerned with what he has termed dissipative structures. These, as we noted earlier, are chemical systems which can be maintained in steady states far from their thermodynamic equilibrium. Randomly occurring fluctuations within the system can move the system to higher degrees of ordering. The possibility of this kind of change is not remote. Indeed it appears that it could occur under a sufficiently wide range of circumstances for it to become probable if not certain. Since life – a highly complex dissipative structure – is a characteristic of the highest levels of molecular organization it is plausible to suppose that its appearance is the natural outcome of the random processes which Monod describes. If this is so, it could be seen as evidence of the working out of a purpose. Eigen's work too shows that random (stochastic) models for molecular systems can behave in surprising ways. For example, even when all members of a system of some kind have equal chances of long-term survival one of them may very quickly achieve dominance. The book by Eigen and Winkler, entitled *Laws of the Game*,[35] illustrates many of these ideas by constructing games which readers can play in order to convince themselves of the often surprising consequences of chance processes. All of this is subject matter for a later chapter but the conclusion to which it leads can be anticipated and summed up in the words of Eigen.

> We may furthermore conclude that the evolution of life, if it is based on a derivable physical principle, must be considered an *inevitable* process despite its indeterminate course. . . . The models treated . . . and the experiments discussed . . . (earlier in this article) indicate that it is not only inevitable 'in principle' but also sufficiently probable within a realistic span of time.[36]

Peacocke goes on to see the subtle interplay of chance and law (necessity) as going beyond mere mechanics and partaking of the joy of God in his creation. The images of music and dance are invoked to express the variety and richness of the creation as it moves elegantly and inevitably on its way.

To sum up then, we have seen that Monod posed a serious challenge to theism and Christian belief, in particular. Broadly speaking, and oversimplifying, there appear to be two ways out of the impasse represented by the contributions of MacKay and Peacocke. Both accept Monod's science. One sees chance only as a way of describing our ignorance; in reality all is determined by the will of God; there would be no uncertainty if we were able to see things through God's eyes. The other gives a more fundamental and positive role to chance and sees it as a tool employed by God to achieve his purposes. Whether or not this creates more theological problems than it solves remains to be seen.

There is however, another popular line of reasoning which has not, as far as I am aware, appeared in the Monod debate. If its conclusion is accepted, the chance hypothesis is demolished in one fell swoop. It is simply that such a hypothesis renders the universe as we know it so extremely improbable as to make it virtually impossible. If absence of design is ruled out, the only conclusion left is that the world is the result of a plan. Before we can proceed we must consider the status of this argument.

3

God or Chance

The idea that one can infer something about the origin and purpose of the universe by calculating probabilities has a long history and some distinguished exponents. If this is really possible, the conclusions at which one arrives are clearly relevant to the central question of the last chapter. The mode of reasoning involved has been widely used and deserves a name. We shall call it the *significance test* approach to theism because it bears a strong resemblance to the procedure which statisticians use to test hypotheses. A common version of the argument based on probabilities goes something like this. Let us set up the hypothesis that there is no directing purpose behind the universe so that all change and development is the product of 'blind' chance. We then proceed to calculate the probability that the world (or that aspect of it under consideration) would turn out to be as we find it. If this probability proves to be extremely small we argue that the occurrence of something so rare is totally implausible and hence that the hypothesis on which it was calculated is almost certainly false. The only reasonable alternative then open to us is to postulate a guiding intelligence to account for what has occurred. This procedure is based on the logical disjunction: *either* an extremely rare event has occurred *or* the hypothesis on which the probability was calculated is false. Faced with this choice, the rational thing to do is to prefer the latter alternative.

This kind of approach has been applied both to the details of the creation, such as the sex-ratio in humans or animals, and to fundamental aspects of the whole cosmos, like the appearance of life. As we shall shortly see some characteristics of the world appear to have exceedingly small probabilities on the chance hypothesis. If the logic of the argument set out above is correct, the case for a non-random (i.e. purposive) explanation of the universe, life in it, or whatever, is then overwhelming. An argument based on impeccable logic and precise calculation which sets the question of God's existence (and, to some extent, his nature) beyond all reasonable doubt would, one might suppose, have been grasped with relief by Christian apologists. With the classical arguments tried and found wanting such promising reinforcements on the side of theism clearly demand careful scrutiny. John Hick includes one such argument, due to the physiologist Le Comte du Noüy, in his review of the arguments for the existence of God.[1] He dismisses it on the ground that the calculation of the probability in question is incorrect. This is certainly true but the incorrectness of the calculation in that particular case has no bearing on the validity of the form of the argument in general. It deserves a much more careful scrutiny than Hick was willing, or able, to give it. The same data were considered by Matson and he rejected the theistic conclusion on the ground that it imported the 'principle of insuffient reason' into the argument.[2] Roughly speaking this says that if nothing is known about a set of outcomes, they should be treated as equally likely. This principle, usually associated with the name of Laplace, has fallen into disrepute both because of the difficulty of providing an adequate justification, and because of the absurd conclusions to which it is liable to lead. We shall see in a moment how the assumption enters, but note again that the questionable application of an argument does not destroy its general validity.

John Arbuthnot and divine providence

A celebrated and, possibly, the first example of the significance test argument was propounded in 1710 by Dr John Arbuthnot – a man of many parts, physician to Queen Anne and originator of John Bull. Writing in the *Philosophical Transactions of the Royal Society*, he made the somewhat startling claim that one could infer the action of divine providence from the records of christenings in the London parishes. He begins his paper:

> Among innumerable Footsteps of Divine Providence to be found in the Works of Nature, there is a very remarkable one to be observed in the exact Balance that is maintained, between the Numbers of Men and Women; for by this means is provided, that the Species may never fail, nor perish, since every Male may have its Female, and of a proportionable Age. This Equality of Males and Females is not the Effect of Chance but Divine Providence, working for a good End, which I thus demonstrate.[3]

Arbuthnot's argument is an interesting early example of a significance test. It is not entirely clear or complete by modern standards but its main thrust is unambiguous. He assumes that if sex is determined by chance, then any birth is equally likely to be male or female, and that the outcome of any individual birth will be independent of all others. He first notes (with calculations in support) that in any finite (but large) number of births it is very unlikely that the numbers of each sex will be exactly equal. Nevertheless they will not depart too far from equality and limits within which deviations from equality are almost certain to lie can easily be calculated. In some years one would get an excess of females, in others of males. What one would not expect to find is that the advantage always lay with one sex. Yet if one looks at the records this is precisely what occurred. Arbuthnot had data for London extending over 82 years from 1629 to 1710 and in every one of them there were more boys born than girls. The chance of this happening in any one year is $\frac{1}{2}$ on the random hypothesis; the chance that it happens 82 times in succession is $(\frac{1}{2})^{82}$ (i.e. $\frac{1}{2}$ multiplied by itself 82 times). This is approximately 0.2×10^{-24} which is an extraordinarily small number (1 divided by 5 million million million million). As if this were not evidence enough, Arbuthnot goes on to speculate that the same imbalance would be found over longer periods of time and, not only in London, but all over the world. We may raise our eyebrows at the addition of 'imaginary' data to the argument, though subsequent demographic evidence amply justifies it. He then reaches the triumphant conclusion 'that it is Art, not Chance that governs'. Furthermore, to Arbuthnot's eyes, the deviation was precisely in the direction one would expect from a providential God since males, who seek their food with danger and are more susceptible to disease and more prone to die, need to be produced in larger relative numbers to maintain a proper balance between the sexes. A theological bonus of the argument, so to speak, is that Arbuthnot is able to point out that his results also demonstrate that polygamy is contrary to the law of nature and justice!

This account contains the essential elements of what I have termed the significance test argument. We shall examine its logic in a moment but before doing so we note a crucial assumption which, if rejected, greatly weakens our confidence in the conclusion. The distinction between Art and Chance is not so clear cut as Arbuthnot supposes. According to him it is an essential part of the chance hypothesis that an individual birth is equally likely to be male or female. In the absence of any directing influence he is supposing that, as with the coin that is tossed, both outcomes are equally likely. Suppose, however, that we decompose the chance hypothesis into two parts. Part I says that the sex of any child is determined, at random, and quite independently of any other birth. Part II specifies that in any particular case the chance is one half. Now it could happen that there was some (accidental) biasing mechanism in the process of sex determination which rendered one sex more probable than the other. The chance in Part II would then be something other than one half but the outcome in any case would still be uncertain. The new form of the hypothesis still involves no purposive action, chance still has a central role. Furthermore one could easily find a value for the probability in Part II (about 0.52) which makes the hypothesis entirely compatible with the London data. Is the new hypothesis Art or Chance – or a bit of both? Arbuthnot might well argue it was Art since anything other than an equal chance could only arise by some deliberate act of the Creator. To a modern statistician with a wider knowledge of random processes this would be unconvincing. Regularities, such as constant (but equal) birth rates can perfectly well arise as aggregated phenomena of other random processes at a lower level. In addition, of course, males and females might well be formed in equal numbers at conception but have different survival rates prior to birth (as, indeed, they do afterwards).

John Arbuthnot's argument is thus ill-founded in this particular case but it serves as a prototype of one which has often been used since. His unwitting disciples have commonly reflected on the improbability of the whole cosmos, or the appearance of life in it, and have deduced the presence of the divine will and purpose. Let us consider some further examples.

The state of the universe

According to A. J. Ayer, the celebrated mathematician John von Neumann advanced 'as an argument in favour of theism the fact that the actual distribution of atoms in the universe was highly improbable'.[4] Whether or not von Neumann had any particular calculation in mind or whether he committed it to paper, I have been unable to discover but Paul Davies has examined the same question in an article 'Chance or choice; is the Universe an accident?'[5] This poses Arbuthnot's question in modern guise and on the grand scale. Davies' article is in the form of a review but it sets out admirably the nature of the problem at a level of sophistication which deters the over-eager from drawing the facile conclusions which von Neumann's remark might invite. Moreover Davies concentrates on setting out some of the possibilities with only the briefest indication of their metaphysical implications.

In Davies' account there are two aspects to the problem. The first concerns the distribution and variety of matter in the universe. The question here is: is the matter in the universe very much what one would expect, given our knowledge of the state of things when the universe began? If not, then the significance test argument could be used to infer that there must have been some intervention in order to bring about something so inherently improbable.

The favoured theory of the origin of the universe now seems to be that it began with a violent explosion about fifteen billion years ago when the primeval material was in a chaotic state. We also know from the second law of thermodynamics that the universe is 'running down' in the sense that the average degree of disorder is increasing. The end-point of this process is seen by physicists at total absorption of the universe in a 'black hole'. In spite of all this the universe as we know it contains a high degree of order. How did this order arise out of the primeval chaos when the stream of development is apparently running strongly in the opposite direction? It appears highly improbable and from one point of view it is. But one can point out that the second law is a statistical law and hence prescribes only the average course of events. This does not preclude the possibility that highly improbable patterns might arise by chance just as eddies in a stream may temporarily allow water to flow against the direction of the current. In fact Davies quotes a calculation of Boltzmann to the effect that one would only expect to find a random fluctuation from the average such as we now observe once in every 10^{80} years. A thousand years may be as a day in the sight of God but such an enormous number defies comprehension. Even allowing for considerable uncertainty in the age of the universe the chance of a variation of the required kind having occurred since its beginning is absolutely negligible. This is the point at which the significance test argument is invoked to infer that there must have been a deliberate input of information at an early stage which served as a programme (in the computing sense) to engineer the highly structured world we inhabit.

Once again, however, the simple dichotomy of design or chance is not as clear cut as the argument requires. Davies explains how the initial violent explosion of the 'big bang' was able, in a sense, to wind up the universe so introducing a degree of order into the cosmos which has been unwinding ever since. Thus in the extreme heat of the initial state it was impossible for all but the simplest entities to exist. By the time it was cool enough for more complex elements to form, the density and temperature had fallen too far for the reactions to make much headway. For the most part the transformation of matter did not get beyond helium, and ever since change has been proceeding slowly inside the stars. The initial expansion and consequent cooling of the universe thus generated a good deal of order represented by large quantities of just a few of the possible elements. This represents the store of order (information) on which subsequent development has drawn. (Later we shall meet other examples and ways where order may arise from chaos.) Making allowance for this Davies concludes, without putting a figure on the probability, that there is nothing very special about the universe in that what we see, in terms of its chemical make-up, is similar to what one would have expected given the initial conditions. In this case, therefore, the method fails to provide evidence for purpose. There is a somewhat subtler use of the significance test here than was used by Arbuthnot. The claim does not concern the probability of the universe exactly as we have it but with a class of *equivalent* outcomes which collectively have a certain probability. This Davies judges to be high enough to be in conformity with the random hypothesis. (It may be argued that chance could not account for the initial explosion but that is part of another argument to which we come at the end of the chapter.) We shall see the significance of this development of the argument later.

If the first aspect is concerned with the distribution of matter and the mix of chemicals, the second arises in connection with gravity. Gravitational forces control the expansion of the universe and mould the matter of the universe into the shapes and patterns which we witness. It would appear that there is more uniformity in the scheme of things than one might have expected. The structure of the world, and hence its ability to support life, is critically dependent on the universe having begun in an extremely smooth and regular condition which may be judged *a priori* to be highly improbable. Again, no numerical calculation can be made, but the qualitative judgment that something very unlikely has occurred amounts to an application of the significance test argument to reject the hypothesis that the initial state was entirely random. The alternative, that the beginning was planned, then seems inescapable.

The origin of life

When we move from the origin of the universe to that of life on this planet we enter a field where, it is claimed, reasonably precise calculations can be made. We have already encountered the argument of Le Comte du Noüy[6] which figures in most subsequent discussions of the cosmological argument for the existence of God. More recently Hoyle and Wickramasinghe have given their own version of the argument in their book, *Evolution from Space*.[7] As the title indicates, it is primarily concerned with the alleged inadequacies of Darwin's evolutionary theory and with the authors' own theory that the origin of life on earth was due to the arrival on earth of genes from space. In part, the case rests on calculations which purport to show that the universe is simply not old enough for life to have evolved to its present state if the random processes of mutation and natural selection were solely responsible. The arrival at a probability of 1 in $10^{40,000}$ of life arising by chance led a *Methodist Recorder* staff writer to use the headline: 'Sceptical scientists reach the inescapable conclusion; There *must* be a God.'[8] Hoyle and Wickramasinghe, in fact, made a number of calculations. They considered, for example, the structure of the haemoglobin molecule and of the surprising discovery of this kind of molecule in legumes in which it has no apparent use. The alpha-chain in man is a chain of 141 amino acids, and there are 20 such acids to choose from. The total number of chains which it would be possible to construct is thus $(20)^{141}$. Of these, perhaps, as many as 80 might be capable of performing the functions of haemoglobin. Even if we err on the generous side and allow that 100 different compositions might serve, the chance that a chain formed at random would have the required probability is about 1 in 2.8×10^{181}. In the primeval 'soup', in which the raw materials are commonly assumed to have been present, there would, of course, have been vast numbers of building blocks and many opportunities for molecules of haemoglobin to form, but nothing like enough to render the probability of one acceptable molecule appearing, somewhere at some time non-negligible: 2.8×10^{181} is a number vastly greater than the number of atoms in the known universe. When we recall that the components of haemoglobin would be confined to a rather special kind of molecule in a tiny corner of the universe, it is clear that the chance of the random formation of haemoglobin is virtually impossible.

The example quoted by du Noüy is similar and concerns a simple protein molecule of 2000 atoms.[9] The probability of a configuration of atoms of the right kind turns out to be 1 in 5×10^{320}. If a volume of 'raw material' equal to the earth was shaken 500 trillion times per second it would take 10^{243} billions of years to form a single molecule and this is vastly in excess of the age of the universe. Hoyle and Wickramasinghe's calculation quoted by the *Methodist Recorder* concerns the enzymes which act as catalysts in biological reactions. An enzyme is a sequence of 20 amino acids, and in order to function it must have a suitable surface shape. The authors estimate the probability of obtaining a suitable backbone as no more than 1 in 10^{15}, and that of obtaining the appropriate active site as 1 in 10^5. This gives a chance of 1 in 10^{20} of obtaining the required enzyme. Since there are about 2000 enzymes in all, Hoyle and Wickramasinghe conclude that the chance of the complete set arising by chance as 1 in $10^{40,000}$: 'an outrageously small probability that could not be faced even if the whole universe consisted of organic soup.'[10]

These breathtakingly small probabilities pose two questions which must be answered before we can follow their proponents to belief in God, antichance or whatever else we choose to call the origin of the otherwise inexplicable. The first, already met with in Arbuthnot's case, is whether or not the calculations have been correctly carried out. In other words are there any other means by which purely chance processes could produce life, or the universe, with non-negligible probabilities? The second question concerns the legitimacy of the inference that is made from the highly improbable event to the existence of a directing purpose. That is, can we ever infer on the basis of correctly calculated probabilities, which turn out to be very small, that 'Art not Chance' rules?

There are, in fact, good reasons for questioning the calculations which we have just presented. They rest on a very simple and highly implausible model of how complex molecules are formed from simpler ones. It is as though the vast number of amino acids were like balls of different colours mixed in a large bag. We then have to imagine balls being drawn at random and linked together in a chain of fixed length. It has been pointed out, by Hick[11] among others, that biologists do not believe that chains are formed by this kind of process. Instead, complex molecules are built up in stages from smaller subsystems and the determination of the relevant probabilities is then a much more complicated proposition. Indeed, as we have already noted, Eigen[12] has asserted that the emergence of life may be almost certain given the initial composition and conditions of the universe. Nicolis and Prigogine's *Self Organization in Non-Equilibrium Systems*[13] is a highly technical account of such processes which will convince even the lay reader that the matter is far from simple. Even, therefore, if there is an element of chance in the formation of complex molecules and, ultimately, of life, it is by no means obvious that the chance of its occurrence is as small as some of the simplistic and highly publicized calculations might suggest.

Whatever may be the status of these particular calculations, it is nevertheless a matter of considerable interest to know whether calculations of this kind are in any way relevant to the point at issue. If they are, then it is obviously desirable to refine the method of calculation. If they are not, then such investigations are a waste of time.

Inference from small probabilities

Let us imagine that we have performed a probability calculation which gives an accurate estimate of the probability of some naturally occurring phenomenon, and that this probability turns out to be extremely small. Then according to the significance test argument we are entitled to reject the hypothesis on which the probability was calculated and infer the existence of some guiding purpose directing the course of events. However compelling this argument might seem at first sight, it is easy to demonstrate its absurdity in the form just stated. To do this we shall imagine an experiment with a well-shuffled pack of playing cards. Statisticians frequently resort to such devices which are apt to lend an air of artificiality or, even, frivolity to the discussion. The reason is that it helps to have a clearly defined situation in which the essentials can be laid bare without the host of qualifications which tend to beset more interesting and realistic situations.

A single card is drawn from the well-shuffled pack of playing cards and it turns out to be the Queen of Hearts. The card is returned to the pack which is then thoroughly shuffled before a second card is drawn. Suppose that this is also the Queen of Hearts. The whole procedure is then repeated, say, ten times in all and on each occasion the same card is drawn. Let us now consider the hypothesis that the pack is a standard one of fifty-two cards and that the shuffling is completely random. If the hypothesis is true then it may easily be shown that what we have observed (ten Queens of Hearts in succession) has a probability of $(1/52)^{10}$ or about 7×10^{-18}; that is seven divided by a million, million, million. This is surely sufficiently small to reject our hypothesis on the significance test principle. But before doing so let us pause to reflect on what our reaction would have been to any other sequence that might have been drawn. Consider, for example, the following sequence which occurred in an actual experiment of this kind:

[10C, KS, 9D, 1C, 1H, 7H, 10C, JH, 5H, 10H.]

There is nothing particularly remarkable about this sequence. It is true that there are five hearts out of the ten cards and the ten of clubs occurred twice but such things commonly happen and it is not likely that the result would raise suspicions, either about the composition of the pack, or the honesty of the dealer. Yet the probability of this sequence is exactly the same as that consisting of ten successive Queens of Hearts, namely 7×10^{-18}. A strict application of the principle ought surely to require us to reject the chance hypothesis in this case also. The absurdity we mentioned now becomes apparent when we recognize that we would have had to reject the hypothesis no matter what the outcome had been! Thus, even if the hypothesis were really true, we would know in advance, without bothering to do the experiment, that it would be rejected.

The reader may be forgiven for feeling a sense of being tricked into accepting a conclusion which is 'obviously' false. The series of ten cards all alike engenders a strong disbelief in the hypothesis of random drawing from a well-shuffled pack whereas we have no such qualms about the observed series. Why is this? Our intuition is right but it is not the very small probability of the ten Queens of Hearts which justifies it.

Before trying to resolve the dilemma which this line of argument poses, let us return to the kind of probability calculations carried out by Hoyle and Wickramasinghe. There we noted that the enzymes which actually exist are but a tiny fraction of those which are theoretically possible. Equally, we could have argued that any other set which might have occurred (and which we might not have been here to observe!) would have had the same small probability and so have provided the same evidence for theism. Thus, whatever had occurred, the same conclusion would have been reached and so we would have a 'proof' of the proposition that in any world with a large number of possibilities the significance test argument would lead to theism.

Clearly something is wrong, and we must seek to identify the source of the trouble. There must, after all, be some rationality in a procedure which has served statisticians well since the early part of this century. Our card drawing experiment provides some clues. There *is* something special about the sequence of ten Queens of Hearts that is lacking in most of the millions of other possible sequences. Whereas there was nothing about the random drawing to cast doubt on the hypothesis, the ten cards all alike strongly suggests a non-standard pack or that the drawer was a trickster. It is not unusual to see card tricks which produce improbable sequences. There is, in fact, a pack which can be bought in which every other card is a Queen of Hearts, and these cards are slightly larger than the others so that they can be easily extracted. It is background knowledge of this kind that makes us suspicious of any sequence with a clear pattern. It is because the Queens of Hearts are *so much more probable* on another hypothesis – that the pack has been 'fixed' – that we feel justified in rejecting the random hypothesis in that case.

This example makes clear that it is not sufficient to look at the probability of the event on the random hypothesis alone, but also at its probability on other hypotheses. In order to reject the chance hypothesis it would seem that the probability ought not only to be small on that hypothesis, but that it ought to be much larger on the alternative hypothesis. But here again there is a difficulty. In the card drawing experiment there is no difficulty in giving credibility to the hypothesis that the pack or the drawer might be 'fixing' the result, so as to give the special outcome a high probability. We know that such things happen and can well believe that they might have done so in this case. If, however, we turn to the question of the origin of life or the universe, then the God hypothesis might be claimed to give all existing phenomena a high probability, if not making them absolutely certain. For if God intended things to be as they are and arranged that they should be so then their happening is in no way surprising. Compared with the virtual impossibility of things being as they are on the chance hypothesis, it still seems that we would be justified in opting for theism. Only if there were no conceivable hypothesis on which the events in question had probabilities appreciably greater than chance predicts would we have grounds for being content that Chance rather than Art ruled. It would thus appear that the significance test argument can be saved provided that we can show that what we observe has a much higher probability on some other hypothesis consistent with theism.

Many, probably most, statisticians would agree that a hypothesis can only be judged by reference to alternatives. Some would want to go farther and argue that the consideration of relative probabilities is not sufficient. We shall pursue this line of argument in a moment. First we note that there are some statisticians who would contend that a significance test can be carried out without reference to any alternatives at all. This view is particularly associated with the name of R. A. Fisher, and Gillies[14] has attempted to provide a philosophical justification for this view (unsuccessful in my opinion). It is instructive to see how they would cope with the dilemma posed by drawing ten Queens of Hearts. The argument now runs that we should look not at individual outcomes but at groups of outcomes. These groups are formed on the basis of similarity of structure. The significance test argument is then applied by reference not to the probability of the individual outcome, but of the class to which it belongs. To do this in the case of the card drawing experiment we would have to identify all outcomes which exhibit the kind of patterns which would arouse our suspicions if they occurred in practice. Thus those consisting all of one suit, all picture cards, sequences in which red and black cards alternated and so on would all belong to the set of 'suspicious' sequences. On the other hand there would be a much greater number which look 'more or less random' such as would occasion no surprise if they were to occur in practice. There would be demarcation problems at the boundary between the two sets, but, wherever it was drawn, the set of 'random' sequences would be very much larger than the 'suspicious' sequences. The hypothesis of randomness would then be judged on the size of the probability of the class into which the observed sequence fell.

In the card drawing illustration the number of cases is too large to list for illustrative purposes, but a simpler example using five coins will, perhaps, make it easier to grasp the point. If five coins are tossed independently there are thirty-two possible sequences which could occur; they are listed below in an obvious notation:

HHHHH, HHHTH, HHTHH, HTHHH, THHHH, HHTTH, HTHTH, THHTH,
HTTHH, THTHH, TTHHH, HTTTH, THTTH, TTHTH, TTTHH, TTTTH,
HHHHT, HHHTT, HHTHT, HTHHT, THHHT, HHTTT, HTHTT, THHTT,
HTTHT, THTHT, TTHHT, HTTTT, THTTT, TTHTT, TTTHT, TTTTT.

With such a small number of cases (compared with the millions of millions in the card drawing experiment) almost any outcome – or none – could be claimed as special in some sense. However, I imagine that most people would agree that the first and last cases are the most suspicious. (HHHHH and TTTTT). Next one might possibly add THTHT and HTHTH. if we agree to regard only 'all heads' or 'all tails' as extreme we would have a 'critical set' with two elements and associated probability 1/16. The probability of a suspicious sequence is thus 1/16 and we would have to decide whether this was small enough to warrant rejecting the hypothesis of unbiased coins fairly tossed. In the card drawing experiment the relevant probability would be that associated with the whole set of suspicious sequences and not simply with a single member of it.

In his *New Scientist* article,[15] Davies used this kind of reasoning in relation to the origin of the universe. Of all the possible universes which could have occurred, one needs to identify those which display sufficient pattern and structure to be regarded as indicative of design and purpose. If the probability attaching to this set is sufficiently small, then one might conclude that the actual universe could not reasonably be attributed to chance.

The crucial question for those who believe that this procedure can be carried out without regard to alternatives arises in the choice of those outcomes which are to be regarded as extreme – the critical set. In our examples with the cards we have imagined the critical set to have been chosen to include just those patterns which seem to be indicative of a faulty pack or sleight of hand in the shuffling. The very arrangements which would occasion surprise are precisely those where we might suspect the intervention of some human agent. In other words the definition of pattern in the outcomes is an implicit way of saying what alternative hypotheses we are willing to entertain. The independence of the method from any notion of alternatives is therefore an illusion. We are back to comparing probabilities implicitly if not explicitly because the critical set is so constructed that its members are, collectively, presumed to have a higher probability on some other hypothesis.

If the atheist might have been encouraged by our dismissal of the significance test argument in its original form he may feel, with justice, that the scales have now been loaded against him. The theist has the great advantage of being able to invoke a God hypothesis according to which the present outcome is, if not certain, then highly probable. The atheist, for his part, has to rely on hypotheses of randomness which, in a complex world, are almost bound to give small probabilities to what we observe. This gives the theist grounds for rejecting the chance hypothesis. To see the force of the problem this poses, let us return to the card drawing experiment and look again at the sequence obtained from an actual drawing. This was obtained from a true pack with adequate shuffling. There is no reason to doubt the random hypothesis on this evidence. But suppose that we are confronted by a strict determinist like Schoffeniels who claims that there is no such thing as chance and that this particular order was pre-determined by some inherent law of nature to which he is privy. He has no difficulty in rejecting the chance hypothesis, which we have happily accepted, because on his hypothesis the observed outcome is certain.

Our unease at accepting the logic of this argument is likely to lie in the feeling that it should not be open to anyone to introduce a hypothesis, however implausible, which has been specially constructed to render the data highly probable. In the case of creation we feel that something is needed more than the relative probabilities of the event under the two hypotheses. Some account, surely, should be taken of the inherent plausibility of the hypothesis. More precisely, of how likely, in some sense, the God (or random) hypothesis is. A. J. Ayer seems to have sensed this in trying to identify the source of his dissatisfaction with von Neumann's argument. He writes: 'I was too diffident or too slow-witted to say more at the time than that I did not find the argument convincing; but thinking about it afterwards I saw that the fallacy lay in a misuse of the concept of probability. Antecedently to experience, we have no more reason to expect an even distribution of atoms than any other.'[16] It is not entirely clear what this means, but in identifying our prior beliefs as relevant to the inference he puts his finger on the crucial weakness of von Neumann's significance test argument which he is rejecting.

In order to bring the issue into sharper focus let us look at a controversial but less fundamental, matter where the significance test argument is often used. Experiments are conducted by parapsychologists to determine whether Extra Sensory Perception (ESP) exists. (We shall have reason to look at this question again in Chapter 5 in connection with the book of Hardy, Harvie and Koestler on *The Challenge of Chance*.[17]) Such experiments present many practical problems because of the need to eliminate all sensory communication between the participants but it is only with the logic of the inference procedure that we are now concerned. We assume, therefore, that if any communication occurs at all it is telepathic. In a typical experiment a subject will be shown a sequence of cards showing letters or familiar objects. Another subject, separated from the first, is then invited to 'guess' what is on each card seen by the first subject. In a sufficiently long series of trials a subject will be liable to get a small number of answers correct, even if he is only guessing, that is, if there is no communication of any kind. Suppose, however, that the second subject scores considerably better than the chance hypothesis predicts. What credence can we then give to the hypothesis that some extra sensory means of communication exists? The statistical approach to this problem described above is to divide the possible outcomes of the experiment into two classes. The division is made in such a way that all outcomes in the critical class represent greater deviations from the random hypothesis (i.e. they are more suspicious) than any of those in the complementary class. Secondly, if the critical class so constructed is very small the probability of an outcome falling in this class is also very small. 'Very small' here means small enough for the experimenter to be willing to reject the hypothesis rather than accept that such a rare event had occurred. All of this, notice, can be done before the experiment is actually carried out.

Suppose next that the experiment is carried out and the outcome observed does, in fact, fall into the critical set. On the significance test principle we are then entitled to reject the hypothesis of guessing in favour of ESP. Many such experiments have been carried out and sometimes highly significant results have been obtained. Let us assume that checks have always been made to exclude all possible sensory means of communication to everyone's satisfaction. In the face of such evidence there are still people who refuse to accept the conclusion that ESP occurs. Can such a stance be justified on rational grounds or is it purely an act of prejudice? Those who would claim that their refusal to accept the results is rational would do so on the ground that the phenomenon was so much at variance with scientific knowledge that there *must* be some other explanation. Put another way, they are saying that *a priori* ESP is impossible, or virtually so. No amount of evidence can convince a person who is absolutely sure that something is impossible.

Inference using prior probabilities

In the last paragraph we have come to the boundary between objective probabilities which, in principle, can be calculated on clearly expressed principles to everyone's satisfaction, and the subjective question of what it is reasonable to believe. Some statisticians would argue that their job is done when the boundary is reached. Having calculated statistical probabilities relevant to the question and provided guidelines for their interpretation it is up to the user to form his beliefs in the light of the evidence. For them the significance test argument in its relative form provides a rational way to proceed. If an event has a very small probability on the random hypothesis but a very much larger (though possibly still small, absolutely) probability on some other alternative, then there is sufficient reason to reject randomness. Others, however, would maintain that statistical science should be interpreted more broadly to include what it is reasonable to believe in the light of all the evidence. They consider that differing amounts of objective evidence justify different strengths of belief which may be legitimately quantified, and that it is the business of statisticians to do this. This approach to statistical inference goes back to Laplace but has been given firmer foundation by, among others, Savage and de Finetti.[18]

To accept this approach yields great benefits in that we can begin to talk about the probability of a hypothesis being true. However, the price to be paid is high in that a degree of objectivity has to be sacrificed. The probabilities occurring in our discussion thus far have been based on considerations of symmetry, independence and frequency. When we speak of the probability of ten Queens of Hearts we are referring to a well-defined event and to a probability which, in principle, at least, could be estimated empirically as a relative frequency by repeated shuffling and drawing. When we move into the realm of degrees of belief we are talking about the mental state of an individual. The difference is that between the probabilities of the lottery and those of horse racing. Betting odds quoted by bookmakers are numerical degrees of belief in the outcomes of horse races and they could not be estimated by relative frequencies even in principle because the events in question are unique and cannot be repeated. If we could establish a calculus appropriate to degrees of belief then the way is open to bring the ESP sceptic within the realm of rational discourse.

It is very common for objective probabilities to be mistakenly interpreted as measures of belief. Hoyle and Wickranasinghe fall into the trap when interpreting their probability of 1 in $10^{40,000}$. They write:

Any theory with a probability of being correct that is larger than one part in $10^{40,000}$ must be judged superior to random shuffling. The theory that life was assembled by an intelligence has, we believe, a probability vastly higher than one part in $10^{40,000}$ of being the correct explanation of the many curious facts discussed in preceding chapters.[19]

Whatever their beliefs may be there is no logical justification for turning the probability of an event into that of a hypothesis. One part in $10^{40,000}$ is the chance, on certain assumptions, of 2000 specific enzymes being constructed from 20 amino acids. It is not the probability that the random hypothesis is true. The means by which we can pass from the probability of an event to that of a hypothesis is provided by Bayes' theorem. Thomas Bayes was an eighteenth-century Presbyterian minister whose celebrated theorem has provided the launching pad for an important branch of modern statistics.

To see what this involves, consider a simple example suggested by a problem in medical diagnosis. A patient presents herself to a doctor who, after an examination, is convinced that she is suffering from one of two conditions, A or B. A is a rare condition and there is extensive evidence, based on post-mortem examinations, that B occurs 100 times as frequently as A. Without further information it would then be reasonable to assume that the patient has B and treat her accordingly. The doctor, however, is able to obtain additional evidence by asking for a hospital test to see whether the patient has a blood condition S. A positive result is possible with either condition but much more likely if A is present; one in two patients with A give a positive result but only one in 500 of those with B. Suppose the patient turns out to have S; the question is how to combine these pieces of information to help diagnose the disease.

We first show how to solve the problem in the general case and then return later to consider these particular numerical values. It helps to introduce some notation as follows. Let $P(A)$ be the proportion of those patients known to be suffering from one or other condition that actually have A; $P(B)$ is the proportion who have B and because they must have one or the other $P(A) + P(B) = 1$. Next let $P(S$ given $A)$ be the proportion of sufferers from A who have S; $P(S$ given $B)$ is the corresponding proportion among those who have B. What the doctor needs to know is $P(A$ given $S)$ which is the proportion of those with S who have A. This could be interpreted as the probability that a person whose test is positive is suffering from A. If this were greater than one half the doctor would know that A was more likely than B. This proportion may be calculated as follows.

$$P(A \text{ given } S) = \frac{\text{Number who respond positively who are As}}{\text{Total number who respond positively}}$$

To facilitate the argument suppose we have a sample of 1000 people known to have A or B (any other large number can be used without affecting the conclusion). The number who have A will then be 1000P(A) and of these a proportion P(S given A) will show S. Hence the number of As who have S is 1000P(A) × P(S given A). Repeating the argument with B in place of A the number of Bs who have S is 1000P(B) × P(S given B). The total number who respond positively is thus

$$1000P(A) \times P(S \text{ given } A) + 1000P(B) \times P(S \text{ given } B).$$

Substituting these quantities into the expression for P(A given S) above the 1000s cancel and we are left with

$$P(A \text{ given } S) = \frac{P(A) \times P(S \text{ given } A)}{P(A) \times P(S \text{ given } A) + P(B) \times P(S \text{ given } B)}$$

Interpreting the proportions as probabilities we have the simplest version of Bayes' theorem. It shows how probabilities of the kind P(A given S) are related to those of the kind P(S given A). Its relevance to the main concern of this chapter is that if A represents a hypothesis about, for example, the origin of life and S some observed feature of the world, such as the occurrence of a specific set of enzymes, then the formula tells us how to calculate the probability that the hypothesis is true given that S has occurred. But first we return to the doctor's problem.

Since B occurs 100 times to A's once it follows that

$$P(A) = \frac{1}{101} \text{ and } P(B) = \frac{100}{101}$$

Similarly

$$P(S \text{ given } A) = \frac{1}{2} \text{ and } P(S \text{ given } B) = \frac{1}{500}$$

We now have all the ingredients for calculating P(A given S) which is

$$P(A \text{ given } S) = \frac{\dfrac{1}{101} \times \dfrac{1}{2}}{\dfrac{1}{101} \times \dfrac{1}{2} + \dfrac{100}{101} \times \dfrac{1}{500}} = \frac{5}{7}.$$

Thus whereas before the test was made the evidence favoured B the odds have now shifted in favour of A. The rarity of someone with B showing S is more than sufficient to counteract the prior presumption in favour of B.

It is instructive to see how this conclusion compares with those we would have reached using either version of the significance test argument. For this purpose let us consider the credibility of the hypothesis that the patient has B. For the first version we need the probability of the data (S, in this case) given that the patient has B. This is P(S given B) which at 1/500 would seem to give strong reason for rejecting B. If we made Hoyle and Wickramasinghe's error of interpreting 1/500 as the probability that B was correct we would still have found the evidence favouring A, but the probability of A would have been 499/500 instead of the correct value of 5/7. That is we should have grossly misjudged the weight of evidence in favour of A. In the second version of the significance test argument we would have compared P(S given A) with P(S given B) since we would then only be justified in rejecting B if P(S given B) is small relative to P(S given A). Here again we would be confident in rejecting B since S is 250 times as likely on A as B. It is perfectly possible to have the significance test arguments leading to the opposite conclusion to Bayes' formula. To see this it is only necessary to change P(A) to 1/301, say, when we find

$$P(A \text{ given } S) = \frac{5}{11} \; .$$

In this case the evidence favours B but the significance test arguments are unchanged in rejecting B.

All of this may appear to be a piece of statistical sleight of hand but, as this example was designed to show, it rests only on a straightforward and unexceptional enumeration of cases. The example was admittedly contrived to illustrate a point in a striking fashion but its validity is quite general.

It now seems that the way is clear to express a rational degree of belief in ESP or the existence of God but, unfortunately one obstacle still remains. Our medical illustration is inadequate in one crucial respect. All of the probabilities appearing in the formula were objective probabilities estimated empirically as proportions. In particular it was possible to estimate the *prior probabilities* P(A) and P(B), from the known incidence of the conditions in the population. Likewise P(A given S) was a relative frequency.

In the application to which we are leading up, the prior probabilities are measures of degrees of belief and cannot be estimated from relative frequencies. Either ESP exists or it does not and there is no conceivable way of examining a large sample of 'worlds' to see in what proportion it occurs. The same is true of God. If it is legitimate to insert any numerical values for P(A) and P(B) it is clear that they must be subjective estimates arrived at by some kind of introspection. As such they will vary from person to person and there is no guarantee that there will be any measure of agreement.

On the question of the legitimacy of using Bayes' formula for subjective (or personal) probabilities it is clear that the arguments based on numbers of cases will not work. Fortunately it may be shown that the basic rules governing the combination of frequency probabilities provide a coherent way of combining probabilities defined in any way whatsoever. In fact, modern treatments of probability theory regard probabilities as undefined quantities subject to certain simple and unexceptional axioms. It is a theory, not about how probability should be measured, but about how probabilities should be manipulated in a coherent fashion. Bayes' theorem thus holds for all kinds of probabilities and for degrees of belief in particular. The theory does not provide a means of assigning numerical values for subjective probabilities.[20] It is therefore not capable, by itself, of providing us with a value for the probability that God or ESP exists. What it does enable us to do is to say *how prior beliefs should be changed by evidence*. To see how this comes about we return to Bayes' formula. Corresponding to the expression for P(A given S) there is a similar expression for P(B given S) obtained by interchanging A and B. Forming the ratio we then have

$$\frac{P(A \text{ given } S)}{P(B \text{ given } S)} = \frac{P(A)}{P(B)} \times \frac{P(S \text{ given } A)}{P(S \text{ given } B)}$$

The three factors in this equation are referred to as 'odds ratios' since they express the probability of one event as a multiple of the other. Thus P(A)/P(B) tells us how much more likely A was than B before S is observed. The factor P(S given A)/P(S given B) converts the prior odds into the posterior odds and is known technically as the likelihood ratio. In the medical example

$$\frac{P(A)}{P(B)} = \frac{1}{100} \text{ and } \frac{P(A \text{ given } S)}{P(B \text{ given } S)} = \frac{5}{2}$$

The likelihood ratio is

$$\frac{P(S \text{ given } A)}{P(S \text{ given } B)} = 250$$

which converts the former into the latter. It is this ratio which provides the link with the second version of the significance test argument which, we claimed, should be based on a comparison of the probability of the outcome under the hypothesis being tested with that under the alternative. We now see that it is precisely this ratio which determines how our beliefs ought to change. If a person insists on assigning a zero prior probability to some hypothesis, then no amount of empirical evidence can move him. If, however, he is prepared to allow some probability, no matter how small, then given sufficient evidence, his view can be changed.

Let us now attempt to apply these ideas to such questions as the origin of the universe and of life on earth. The symbols appearing in Bayes' theorem can be given different meanings as follows. Let

$$\text{A be : there is a God,} \qquad \text{B be : there is not}$$

and let S refer to some observable characteristic of the world such as the appearance of life on this planet whose probability we suppose can be calculated to everyone's satisfaction. Then, provided that we can assign numerical values to $P(A)$ and $P(B)$, the formula enables us to compute $P(A \text{ given } S)$ – the probability that God exists given that S has occurred. The prior probabilities are subjective, but the formula can be used to delineate the circumstances in which the evidence would justify belief in God. For example, suppose that the matter is being considered by an extreme sceptic who is only prepared to allow a prior chance of 1 in 50,000 to the existence of God. Let us suppose that S can be taken as certain *if* God exists on the grounds that he can bring about whatever he desires. (The essence of the argument does not depend on this particular value for $P(S \text{ given } A)$.) The other probability required is that of S given that God does not exist and chance rules. If S refers to the existence of the 2000 enzymes constructed from 20 amino acids, Hoyle and Wickramasinghe estimated the probability of this set as 1 in $10^{40,000}$.[21] Leaving aside the serious doubts we have about the legitimacy of this calculation, let us take it at its face value. We then have the following numerical values for the various probabilities.

$$P(A) = \frac{1}{50,000} \, , \qquad P(B) = \frac{49,999}{50,000} \, ,$$

$$P(S \text{ given } A) = 1 \, , \qquad P(S \text{ given } B) = \frac{1}{10^{40,000}} \, .$$

Bayes' formula now gives

$$P(A \text{ given } S) = \frac{\dfrac{1}{50{,}000}}{\dfrac{1}{50{,}000} + \dfrac{49{,}999}{50{,}000} \times \dfrac{1}{10^{40{,}000}}} = 1 - \frac{5}{10^{39{,}996}} \text{ nearly.}$$

This is so close to one that we could regard God's existence as proved beyond all reasonable doubt. The initial very long odds against his existence are completely swamped by the tiny probability of S on the chance hypothesis. Furthermore it is clear that we could have allowed vastly greater prior odds against A without materially altering the conclusion. Thus, although there is no way of arriving objectively at a value for $P(A)$ it is clear that the prior odds against God's existence would have to be absurdly small before atheism would have any credibility whatsoever.

Although the logic of the argument we have finally arrived at is perfectly sound, there is still a serious flaw in its application. The atheist still has one further card to play. The trouble lies in our too ready acceptance of the dichotomy 'God exists'/'He does not'. The statement 'God exists' is, of course, susceptible of many interpretations. One could easily sub-divide the statement – A – 'God exists' – into many mutually exclusive statements of a more elaborate kind called $A_1, A_2, A_3, \ldots$ and so on. For each of these there would be a possibly different value of $P(S \text{ given } A_i)$ according to what capabilities and intentions A_i implies. However, if we merely wish to investigate the probability that a God of some kind exists we can do this by combining the events A_1, A_2 etc. into a composite event A. The real flaw in the argument presented above lies with the hypothesis B which says that what we observe is the result of chance. I doubt whether any ultimate meaning can be given to this hypothesis, but let us ignore this objection. What is certainly true is that there is not a single unambiguous model for the generation of life, determination of sex or whatever. We noted this in the case of John Arbuthnot's calculation. He assumed that 'Chance' meant that a child was equally likely to be male or female. On his interpretation the weight of evidence for rejecting the hypothesis is overwhelming for any reasonable prior odds. However, we pointed out that 'Chance' need not necessarily require the probability of a male birth to be half. Apparently random effects could well result in it being something other than half. There seemed no reason why it should not be something near to 0.52 in which case the observed record of births is very much as one would expect. There is therefore no need to reject the chance hypothesis and Arbuthnot was simply wrong in the conclusion he drew.

With the origin of life the position is much more difficult. Hoyle and Wickramasinghe's calculation is open to serious doubt like that of Le Comte du Noüy before them. Essentially they enumerated the number of ways in which 2000 enzymes can be formed from 20 amino acids. They make the crucial assumption that all these combinations are equally likely to occur and thus arrive at the extremely small probability for the one particular combination which did occur. Just as John Arbuthnot's birth probability did not have to be $\frac{1}{2}$, so it is perfectly reasonable to imagine that some combinations of amino acids are much more likely than others, as the evidence quoted by Schoffeniels appears to show. Thus even with a model which assumes that enzymes were formed 'all at once' by selecting twenty amino acids in turn and at random one can only arrive at a probability by making some heroic and implausible assumption about all combinations having equal chances of being formed. Beyond that, one can envisage many other random models for enzyme formation.[22] For example, a process of development in which small chains are first formed and then subsequently combine into longer chains can still be random and yet yield very different probabilities for what we observe. The calculations required would need detailed knowledge of biological processes at the micro-level and it is to be hoped that progress can be made by those competent to undertake the work. For our purposes it is sufficient to note the implications of there being the possibility of an indeterminate number of different chance hypotheses.

Suppose there are 'Chance' hypotheses B_1, B_2, B_3, . . . some of which we can specify and the remainder of which have not yet occurred to anyone. For simplicity let us agree that 'God exists' can be taken as a single hypothesis. In this case a more general form of Bayes' theorem is required. It is

$$P(A \text{ given } S) = \frac{P(A)P(S \text{ given } A)}{P(A)P(S \text{ given } A) + P(B_1)P(S \text{ given } B_1) + P(B_2)P(S \text{ given } B_2) + \ldots}$$

It is clear that unless we can identify all the Bs and their associated probabilities $P(A \text{ given } S)$ cannot be determined even if we know the prior probabilities. The root of the difficulty lies in our inability to specify all the Bs. If there is just one such chance hypothesis that we are unaware of such that $P(S \text{ given } B)$ is large, the probability of God's existence could be substantially reduced as a few trial calculations will show.

Hoyle and Wickramasinghe thus commit a double error. First they assume that there is only one B and secondly they confuse $P(S \text{ given } B)$

with the degree of belief P(B given S).

As we have seen Bayes' theorem can be expressed in a different way using odds ratios. Thus our earlier result generalizes to

$$\frac{P(A \text{ given } S)}{P(B_i \text{ given } S)} = \frac{P(A)}{P(B_i)} \times \frac{P(S \text{ given } A)}{P(S \text{ given } B_i)}$$

for all chance hypotheses B_i. A minimal requirement for a reasonable degree of belief in A would thus be that all the likelihood ratios

$$\frac{P(S \text{ given } A)}{P(S \text{ given } B_i)}$$

should be large. Unless we can be sure that our list of chance hypotheses is exhaustive, we can never clinch the argument.

Summary

We have followed a long, technical and somewhat tortuous path to investigate what, at the outset, seemed a straightforward matter. Like Hick and Matson our conclusion is that the enormous odds quoted by Le Comte du Noüy, Hoyle and Wickramasinghe and others do not establish the existence of God beyond reasonable doubt. We cannot therefore dismiss Monod's case out of hand on the grounds that the world as we find it could not have arisen without the guiding hand of God. Unlike the earlier critics we have not been content to simply point out errors of calculation but have aimed to be constructive by showing what kind of probabilistic evidence would be needed to settle the matter. The arguments offered hitherto have repeated John Arbuthnot's mistake of assuming that there was only one 'chance' hypothesis. To 'prove' God's existence by this means we would have to demonstrate that there was no possible chance model which could render the existing state of things reasonably probable. If, as Eigen and others claim, the emergence of life in some form is virtually certain even though chance plays a big part in the path by which that end is reached, then the prospects for obtaining the required 'proof' on that evidence are bleak. My own view is that it will never be possible to assess the credibility of theism by arguments of the significance test type. And, if it were, a more satisfying account of how God acts, hinted at in the last chapter and to be developed in what follows, would have to be abandoned.

Three further views

Although I have been highly critical of the various probability calculations purporting to establish hypotheses of the kind 'God exists' or the 'sex ratio is divinely determined', I have also shown that calculations can be made which are relevant to such questions. In particular Bayes' formula shows how prior beliefs should be changed in the light of evidence. The key term in that formula is the likelihood ratio which involves probabilities of events which can, in principle, be found. If it could be shown that all conceivable non-theistic hypotheses led to very low probabilities for the data, there would then be grounds for increasing one's degree of belief in theism.

Judging from their writings two authors would object to this conclusion. Mellor[23] argues that probability theory is inapplicable to such questions and hence that any conclusions reached by this method are invalid. Swinburne,[24] who rejects some of Mellor's arguments, has gone further than I have in using Bayes' theorem to make probability judgments about propositions such as 'God exists'.

In part Mellor's argument can be accepted. For example, he points out that subjective probabilities like P(A) are not concerned with what is true but with what an individual believes. Hence any argument using Bayes' formula (which he does not mention) cannot yield an absolute probability for the theist's hypothesis. This is why I have emphasized the likelihood ratio as the only part of the argument that can be objectively quantified. He also rejects, as I have done, the crude first form of the significance test argument (though couched in somewhat different terms under the 'bridge-hand fallacy'). For the rest, Mellor's argument seems either incorrect or ambiguous and, as far as I can see, no threat to the conclusions of this chapter. The error is contained in the following passage.

> The basis of the required inference is the following principle. Suppose there are two statistical hypotheses, h and i, and i assigns a higher statistical probability than h does to some piece of evidence e. Then on the evidence e, if we may infer anything about the inductive probabilities of h and i, it is that i is more probable than h . . .[25]

The statistical probability that h assigns to e is, in our notation P(e given h) and similarly for P(e given i). The inductive probability of h on the evidence e is what we would denote by P(h given e). Hence translated into our notation Mellor is saying that if

$$P(e \text{ given } i) \text{ is greater than } P(e \text{ given } h)$$

then

$$P(i \text{ given } e) \text{ is greater than } P(h \text{ given } i).$$

It follows at once from Bayes' formula that this is not necessarily so. According to the formula

$$\frac{P(i \text{ given } e)}{P(h \text{ given } e)} = \frac{P(i)}{P(h)} \frac{P(e \text{ given } i)}{P(e \text{ given } h)} .$$

To see the fallacy suppose that

$$\frac{P(i)}{P(h)} = \frac{1}{4} \text{ and } \frac{P(e \text{ given } i)}{P(e \text{ given } h)} = 2$$

then, although P(e given i) is twice as large as P(e given h), P(i given e) is only half as large as P(h given e) which contradicts Mellor's assertion. If the reader has felt the technical aspects of this chapter over-taxing it is salutary to note how Mellor's attempt to express the argument in purely verbal terms led to an elementary mistake.

However, this does not demolish Mellor's case because his point is that even if his logic were correct it would not be possible to implement it because the hypotheses here are not statistical but 'cosmic'. He seems to be saying that a probability like P(e given i) is meaningless when i refers to a cosmic hypothesis. To determine such a probability, he says, the event in question must be, at least in principle, repeatable. His denial that this is the case is difficult to follow because we are here concerned with events like 'in every year in a certain period in London there were more male than female births'. There is no difficulty here in conceiving of repetition and the calculation is straightforward in principle. There is evidence in Mellor's article that he is confusing the probability P(e *and* i) with P(e *given* i). The two are related by

$$P(e \text{ *and* } i) = P(i) \times P(e \text{ *given* } i).$$

If Mellor were really referring to the left hand probability one could accept the difficulty, if not the absurdity, of assigning a probability to an event such as 'there is a god *and* the world is as we find it'. But if we decompose it as above into two probabilities, P(i) concerning the existence of God, and P(e *given* i) concerning the state of the world *given* God exists, the difficulty is clarified. P(i) is subjective and for reasons set out above this means that P(e *and* i) cannot be objectively determined. There is no obvious reason, however, why the same sort of objection should apply to P(e *given* i). Further evidence that Mellor may have been thinking of P(e *and* i) rather than P(e *given* i) is found in the fact that his original statement would have been correct had this substitution been made.

Swinburne has used probability arguments, and Bayes' theorem in particular, to make inferences about God's existence.[26] In his case he is not considering events for which statistical probabilities can be calculated. The 'e' or 'S' in his argument are pieces of evidence of a qualitative kind such as the existence of undeserved suffering. In consequence he has to use weaker forms of argument directed to showing whether a certain kind of evidence increases the probability of God's existence or makes it more likely than not. When used in this mode the approach, originating with Carnap, is called confirmation theory. It is not directly relevant to the theme of this chapter but since Mellor's attack is on the use of probability arguments of any kind, Swinburne's reply is relevant.

His first point is that it *is* possible to say something about the conditional probability P(e given h), and with this I agree. The second appears to be based on a misunderstanding. He supposes Mellor to be saying that one must not only know the conditional probability P(e given i) for the e that has actually occurred, but also for all other events that might have occurred. This is certainly true if one is aiming to construct a critical set because the probability associated with the set cannot be determined otherwise. But it is not a valid criticism of the use of Bayes' theorem. The only conditional probability involved there is the one concerning what has actually happened and not those relating to what might have happened. Indeed it is a central tenet of the Bayesian approach that the inference should not depend on the probabilities of events that have not occurred. There is no need for Swinburne to defend himself on this count since he does not use the significance test approach.

Swinburne does not deal with the more substantial criticism made by Mellor concerning the prior probabilities of the kind P(i) and hence of the posterior probabilities on which everything rests. Possibly this is because Swinburne does not think of them as subjective. He argues that there are objective criteria which bear upon prior probabilities. For example, a simple hypothesis has an intrinsic probability that is higher than that of a complex hypothesis. I do not find this convincing nor do I find it easy to see how to assess the probability P(e) which appears in Swinburne's (equivalent) version of Bayes theorem.

None of these arguments affects our conclusions unless one allows Mellor's claim that conditional probabilities of the form P(e given i) are incoherent when i is a cosmic hypothesis. In the examples we have discussed there seems to be no force in this objection.

In *The Accidental Universe* Paul Davies[27] draws attention to the remarkable coincidences in the fundamental constants of the universe which have combined to produce the world as we know it. These are made the more remarkable by the fact that quite small variations in the initial conditions would have produced quite different courses of evolution from that which has actually occurred. For intelligent beings to have appeared capable of reasoning about their origins and destiny it apparently required such a delicate adjustment of the initial conditions, that it is scarcely credible that this happy conjunction could have arisen without some prior intention. It is difficult to escape the conclusion, as Davies puts it, that 'something is going on'. The alternative seems too improbable to contemplate. It is not at all clear that it is meaningful to talk about probabilities in this context (as Mellor argued) but it is difficult to deny that it is the sheer improbability, in some sense, of these coincidences that seems to compel our belief in some idea of purpose behind it all. Are we justified in this conclusion?

At first sight it appears to be another instance of the significance test argument. In essence we are saying that if, in the absence of a god, the basic constants, like the speed of light, Newton's gravitational constant, the charge on a proton and such like – were selected 'at random' in some giant lottery then what has occurred is extremely improbable. Admittedly it is difficult to see how we could go about assigning a number to the probability but it would be very difficult to argue that it could be other than very small indeed. We are thus faced with the classical choice: either an extremely rare event has occurred or the 'coincidences' were planned. However, there is an important distinction between this case and the others that we have discussed. In all the examples of this chapter the initial conditions were taken as given. The events whose small probabilities were alleged to provide evidence for theism were all consequences of those initial conditions. We were, in effect, saying: given an initial state of the universe such as we believe to have existed in the beginning is it likely that life, for example, would have appeared purely by chance and without outside control? In so far as we understand the physics and biology of cosmic evolution it is possible, in principle, to calculate the probabilities of such events which have actually occurred. The 'cosmic' hypothesis with which Davies is concerned is of a different order altogether and it is extremely difficult to imagine any theoretical framework within which one could begin to assess the magnitude of probabilities. I do not think, therefore, that the line of reasoning developed in the body of the chapter can be applied to cases such as this, and in this I am in agreement with Mellor.

It is interesting, nevertheless, to set aside such objections to see where the argument will lead if we allow that it is meaningful to use probabilities in this context. Davies mentioned two lines of argument which have been used to show that these (apparently) highly unlikely coincidences do not require a belief in some guiding power with a purpose for the creation. One is to suppose that there is not one universe but many, perhaps infinitely many. These could exist simultaneously or sequentially – as one universe fades into extinction another may be born. If the initial conditions are, in fact, a purely chance collection of physical constants then sooner or later a universe will appear in which the conditions are just right for a universe such as ours. We have noted the possibility of this kind of argument before (in Chapter 2). It is certainly a possible explanation though it strains the imagination to the limit and requires the use of words in contexts in which their meaning becomes so fluid as to undermine the very reasoning which they are trying to convey. Indeed, it is arguable that it is more difficult to believe in the multiplicity of universes than in the coincidences which they were introduced to explain.

The second line of argument is more subtle and concerns what is known as the anthropic principle. This requires that, in reasoning about these improbabilities, we should reckon with our own existence without which there could be no speculation at all. In the weak form it says that what we can expect to observe is constrained by the conditions which are necessary for our existence as observers. That is, if a particular set of physical constants is necessary for intelligent life to appear, then it is not at all surprising that in a universe containing living beings that just these coincidences should be observed. If they were not, there would be no one to observe them! The so-called strong form of the principle is really a quite different principle altogether. It says that the universe must be such as to allow the creation of observers within it at some stage in its evolution. This is essentially the same as saying that the universe exists with ourselves in it because God intended it to be so. In its neutral form it really offers no explanation at all and seems to be without rational basis. The theistic version does, at least, have the merit of claiming other kinds of evidence in its support.

The weak form of the anthropic principle deserves more careful examination. This is another instance where a modicum of symbolism is a great aid to clarity. We are concerned with two propositions

A : that the initial conditions and laws of physics were as we now know them to be;

B : that we exist.

By the rules of probability theory, we may write down the following relationship between certain probabilities relating to these two events. Thus

$$P(A \text{ given } B) = \frac{P(A)P(B \text{ given } A)}{P(B)}$$

where, as before, $P(-)$ stands for the probability of the event described in the brackets. Now $P(B)$ can be expressed as

$$P(A)P(B \text{ given } A) + P(\bar{A})P(B \text{ given } \bar{A})$$

where $\bar{A}$ means 'not-A'. If only a very narrow range of initial conditions, represented here by A, is compatible with our appearance, we may surmise that $P(B \text{ given } \bar{A})$ is negligble. Hence *whatever the value of $P(A)$* the denominator in the expression for $P(A \text{ given } B)$ above will be only slightly larger than the numerator with the effect that $P(A \text{ given } B)$ is likely to be close to one.

The claim that we are considering can now be expressed as follows. Although the probability of obtaining the right initial conditions in the absence of a directing purpose, $P(A)$, may be extremely small, the probability of the same event, when we take our own existence into account, $P(A \text{ given } B)$, is not. If the significance test argument were to be used at all, it should therefore be applied to $P(A \text{ given } B)$ which takes account of all the facts. Since this is certainly not small there is no need to invoke purposive action.

This argument is fallacious because there are no grounds for applying the significance test approach to probabilities like $P(A \text{ given } B)$. The test requires the probability to be calculated on the assumption that everything happens 'by chance'. Chance enters the calculation at two points – in the determination of the initial conditions and in the subsequent appearance of life. The second of these is not at issue since the question only concerns whether the initial state was divinely determined. But we have just shown that $P(A \text{ given } B)$ is hardly affected by the value of $P(A)$, which is the only part of the calculation concerned with initial conditions. The value of $P(A \text{ given } B)$ is thus irrelevant for the purpose proposed.

4

Chance and Certainty

Thus far we have been content to treat chance as signifying lack of assignable cause without probing too deeply into its precise nature. This has served us well enough up to the present but, before we can begin to formulate a theology of chance we must look at the foundations more carefully. In particular we must recognize, and seek to understand, the rather subtle and surprising complementarity between chance and determinism. The richness of the English language in nouns and adjectives relating to chance is sufficient to show how deeply and widely the idea is embedded in our thinking. Chance, luck, fortune, uncertainty, probability, risk, likelihood, odds, randomness, unpredictability, caprice, accident, coincidence, lottery, fluke, hazard and fate express a constellation of overlapping and related meanings which are familiar enough. Some, like probability and likelihood, have become technical terms with precise meanings while others, including luck and fate, smack of the occult. We have firmly resisted the personification of chance, though it is difficult to expunge the idea from the language we use. From Milton's 'Chance governs all' to our speaking of 'leaving things to chance' any sentence in which chance appears as a noun is almost bound to mislead in this respect. We have conveniently described the fallacious doctrine that chance is a cause of anything as Tychism after the Greek goddess Tyche. To speak of chance is an admission that no discernable cause is apparent.

Chance and pure chance

It is customary among writers on this topic to distinguish several kinds of chance and we shall do likewise. But first, at the risk of over-simplifying things, let us attempt to specify what all these aspects have in common. *The notion of chance arises whenever a situation exists in which there is more than one possible outcome for an event, and where one cannot predict, with certainty, which outcome will occur.* This embraces the whole spectrum of uncertainty concerning events, from the atomic level to human behaviour.[1] The emission of an alpha particle from a radioactive atom in an interval of time, the time at which a train will arrive, the passing or failing of an examination, the weather next Christmas, the size of the apple crop, are all events which are in some degree unpredictable. In many such cases, some would say in all of them, the uncertainty arises not because the events are, in principle, unpredictable but simply because we are ignorant of the complete causal mechanism leading up to the event. Even if we cannot entirely eliminate uncertainty, we can often reduce it by acquiring further information. The size of the apple crop in my garden will depend on whether I have sprayed the trees at appropriate times, whether there were late frosts at blossom time and so on. Knowledge of all these factors will certainly reduce the uncertainty. A doctor may be uncertain as to whether a patient has diabetes, but after a test has been made the uncertainty may be removed. We may speak of a mid-air collision between two aircraft as an accident because it was not foreseen and certainly not planned. Yet anyone who had available to them the basic data on course and speed could have foreseen what would happen.

Considerations such as these may lead us to the conclusion that chance is simply the reflection in reality of our ignorance. That, in truth, there are no uncaused happenings. If only we were omniscient we would be able to trace the causal links backwards and find a satisfying explanation in deterministic terms. In principle, then, chance would have been banished from the universe and we should be back to the elaborate machine, much more complicated than Newton imagined, but just as predictable. Such a view has many supporters; Karl Popper for example:

> One sometimes hears it said that the movements of the planets obey strict laws, whilst the fall of a die is fortuitous, or subject to chance. In my view the difference lies in the fact that we have so far been able to predict the movement of the planets successfully, but not the individual results of throwing dice. . . . In throwing dice, what we lack is, clearly, sufficient knowledge of initial conditions. With sufficiently precise measurements of initial conditions it would be possible to make predictions in this case also; . . . [2]

Einstein evidently thought the same. Ayer inclines to the opposite view while admitting that it could never be proved. He writes:

> The person who believes in chance, in this absolute sense, can

properly do no more than issue a challenge. He points to certain features of the world and defies anyone to show that they fall entirely in every detail within the grasp of causal laws. But however long he triumphs, there remains, in yet another of the manifold senses of 'chance', the chance that his challenge will eventually be met.[3]

Thus, although the emission of individual particles from a radio-active source appears to be totally unpredictable, it is always possible that some deterministic pattern will eventually be found. I shall argue later that, from a theological point of view, it matters little whether or not all chance can be expressed in deterministic terms. For the moment it is useful to make the distinction between those events which we know could be understood in causal terms if only we had sufficient information, and those for which no causal explanation can be conceived of in the present state of knowledge. In the latter case we shall speak of *pure chance*. The most commonly discussed form of pure chance is that which is encountered at the atomic level but there are others. Ayer speculated that there might well be some irreducible element of pure chance in the deviations from natural laws which we call errors of observation. That is, however precise our measuring instruments, the lack of fit might never be entirely eliminated. Another, and for our purpose, much more important sphere of the operation of pure chance is in human choice. At first sight this appears an absurd statement to make. Although there may be an element of thoughtlessness in some of our choices, most of us would feel that our claim to be regarded as rational creatures makes nonsense of the suggestion that there are no reasons for our decisions. But the real question is: 'Are all our actions, in principle, predictable?' where this question is understood as being addressed not to ourselves, but to anyone but ourselves. If it were possible by making sufficient physiological and psychological observations to predict the actions of an individual, then we could rule out pure chance. We should then be reduced to the level of automata and a strict behaviourism would be the only acceptable psychology. Possibly there are some who do believe that this is the case, but it is extraordinarily difficult to act consistently as if one believed it. The alternative is to suppose that there is a degree, at least, of genuine individual autonomy; that our future choices are not completely determined and that the future is not fixed regardless of what we think or do. Once we allow an element of unpredictability in the interests of preserving human freedom we have introduced pure chance in the sense the term is used here.

Those who believe in Divine providence would add a further source of pure chance in this sense. If there are things which happen in the world through the direct agency of God then they are, almost by definition, unpredictable. The argument which we used to preserve a degree of human freedom would apply with greater force to God himself. Some would argue, as we saw in Chapter 2, that all pure chance events, in the realm of physics at any rate, were the result of the free choices of an all-powerful God. But this is to anticipate the theological discussion of the next chapter. First we must begin an exploration of the technical aspects of chance and, in particular, the complementarity of chance and determinism.

Chaos out of order

A great many chance happenings do not have the character of pure chance. They arise from totally deterministic processes. This goes for many of the randomizing devices which we construct for our own amusement like dice and lotteries. They serve their purpose because we simply do not have the detailed knowledge of the initial conditions, the laws of motion and so forth, and we are thus not able to predict the outcome. It will be helpful to look at such randomizing devices more closely. A simple and instructive example is provided by the counting out rhymes used by children to decide who shall be 'it' in a game. The children stand in a circle; the counter haphazardly picks one child at which to begin and then goes round and round the circle – one word of the rhyme to each child – until the last word is reached. This last child is then 'it'. In a more elaborate version the last child will be left out and the whole procedure repeated with those who remain. The children are thus eliminated from the group one by one until the sole survivor is 'it'. This is not a purely random process. It is no more random than the initial choice, for once the starting point is fixed the final outcome is determined. Knowing the number of children and the number of words it would be a simple matter to predict the outcome with certainty. The method works well enough in practice because, with varying numbers in the group and a large number of words, children do not have time, even if they had the inclination to make the prediction. Put more formally the child chosen is determined by the size of the remainder after the number of words is divided by the number of children.[4]

A very similar method is used to generate what are called pseudo-random numbers. These have many practical applications in science, especially where it is necessary to simulate the behaviour of random processes. The speed with which they can be generated by computers often makes it much easier to experiment with a statistical model of a process rather than to study it theoretically. The aim is to produce a sequence of digits, usually 0, 1, 2, up to 9 in a completely random fashion. This implies that at any stage the next number of the sequence is chosen independently of those that have gone before and in such a way that each of the digits is equally likely to be chosen. Since a computer can only do precisely what it is programmed to do it may seem surprising that it is possible to produce a sequence with the desired properties. How is it that a completely deterministic sequence of numbers can be made to look as if it were the result of pure chance? The clue is provided by the counting out rhyme. We write into the programme a formula which requires the machine to divide one number by another and retain only the remainder. By choosing the formula carefully it turns out that, at least for sequences of moderate length, the series looks just as if it were completely random. The qualification that the sequence be of moderate length is important for if one went on long enough the series would begin to repeat itself and, with sufficient ingenuity, it would be possible to crack the code, recover the formula and hence predict the sequence. The apparent paradox which this state of affairs poses is resolved by realizing that if the observed series is relatively short there will be so little information in it about the law of formation that it will be impossible to deduce enough information about what the formula is to help in prediction. The art of constructing a good random number generator is to find a formula which only repeats itself at intervals which are vastly larger than any sequence that one is likely to want to use in practice.

We have dealt with this example at some length because it beautifully illustrates the point that the question of whether there is such a thing as pure chance is far from simple. If a purely deterministic generator can produce something which, for practical purposes, is indistinguishable from pure chance then we must be very careful about the philosophical and theological implications of invoking pure chance in our attempts at explanation.

The point is so fundamental that we shall mention some other examples. MacKay quotes an interesting example from his own research field.[5] A television screen which is not tuned to a transmitter will appear to be covered with a chaotic array of black and white spots graphically described as 'snow'. This is produced by effectively random signals or 'noise' as it is called. MacKay explains how such an effect can be produced in a purely deterministic manner for use in his own research. In one case the effect is produced in a completely unpredictable way and in the other it is contrived so that it is entirely predictable yet, to the human eye, the two are indistinguishable.

Another instructive example arises with what is called the pooled output. Let us imagine a populous area served by a single telephone exchange. All of the subscribers put calls through the exchange at precisely regular intervals but the intervals vary from one subscriber to another. Some will make calls very frequently and others rather rarely, but all do so in a completely predictable manner (we only choose *equal* intervals for simplicity, the result holds for any fixed pattern). The arrival of calls at the exchange is thus a deterministic process but, viewing the process at the exchange over relatively short intervals, the flow of calls would appear random. The super-position of a large number of individually predictable series thus produces an unpredictable series. If the exchange were to be observed over a sufficiently long time one would be able to pick out regularities and so unscramble the constituent series. In a short interval there is not enough information available to detect any departure from pure randomness. Anyone who has stood at a bus stop served by several routes timed to run at regular intervals will have experienced this phenomenon – and for much the same reasons.

Something rather similar occurs in the case of tossing dice or coins. To oversimplify a little, the fall of the coin depends on how long it is in the air (which depends on the vertical impulse imparted to it) and the speed of revolution (which depends on the amount of spin). The side which falls uppermost is determined by the nearest whole number of revolutions completed. If it is less than half-way through its last revolution it will fall one way; if it is more than half-way through it will fall the other. The number of revolutions is the product of the time in the air and the number of revolutions per second. If these are such as to make the number of revolutions large, the 'remainder' left over when the last complete revolution is made will be virtually unpredictable. With a very gentle toss it might conceivably be possible to control the initial impulse and spin so precisely that one could influence the fall. Under normal conditions the degree of control over impulse and spin would have to be so delicate as to be far beyond what anyone could achieve. Here, then we have a process which, though deterministic, is beyond our ability to control and, hence, to predict.

An even more impressive example of chaos from order is provided by the study of what, in Applied Mathematics, are called dynamical systems. Fluids in motion are examples of such systems. Mathematicians study such processes by setting up equations which purport to describe how the state of the system changes over small intervals of time. The solution of the system of equations then enables them to predict the future behaviour of the fluid. Some such systems behave in a smooth and regular fashion characterized by an approach to equilibrium or, perhaps, a series of oscillations. Other systems behave in an erratic and seemingly unpredictable fashion. Turbulence in the flow of a liquid or in the atmosphere are good examples. One way of incorporating such behaviour into the model is to introduce random perturbations into the equations and so, as it were, super-impose this on the smooth underlying behaviour of a simple deterministic model. Recent research, stemming from the work of Stephen Smale in the 1960s, has shown that it is possible to construct purely deterministic systems which behave in a way remarkably like that of actual physical systems in a state of turbulence. It is therefore possible, in principle, to explain such randomness in purely deterministic terms. This does not make it any easier to predict in practice because, as in the case of coin tossing, the outcomes are extremely sensitive to minor variations in the initial conditions. As Ian Stewart says when speaking of the weather in this connection: 'It's not that we will now be able to predict the weather better: it's more that we have finally begun to understand what makes it unpredictable.'[6] He also raises the possibility that irregularities in the growth of biological populations (and, we might add, social systems) will become explicable in similar terms.

There is one other, closely related, area in which we speak of chance where, in reality, we are dealing with deterministic processes. This concerns those contexts in which we speak of 'coincidence' or accident. Pollard emphasizes the distinction between pure chance and accident. Chance in Pollard's usage is our 'pure chance', and he is thinking of those micro-level phenomena with which quantum mechanics deals. The accidental, in the context of history, 'refers to situations in which two or more chains of events which have no causal connection with each other coincide in such a way as to decide the course of events.'[7] There is no need, of course, to limit the definition to history in the narrow sense. Such happenings are common place in everyday affairs. Thus, for example, an explosion in a coal mine might result from the coincidence of the release of a pocket of methane as a coal face advances, and from a miner illegally lighting a cigarette. Both events belong to separate sequences of happenings in which each stage depends in a direct way on its predecessor. The presence of methane in the seam and the planned advance of the face make the presence of gas in the workings, in due course, a matter of virtual certainty. Similarly, the sequence of events leading to the striking of the match might well be a predictable progression. A person with full knowledge observing either sequence could foresee the particular event which sets off the explosion. What gives the situation its special character is that the two crucial events happen to coincide at a particular point in time and space. An omniscient God presiding over a deterministic world could foresee that, of the immense number of causal chains developing in space and time, these two would interact with disastrous consequences. If it is objected that the presence of a man in one sequence, with freedom to change his mind about lighting the match, destroys the predictability it is only necessary to replace him with a machine having a faulty electrical connection which causes a spark at the crucial moment to preserve the conclusion. Once again then we find evidence that chance, like beauty, 'lies in the eye of the beholder' and not in the nature of the things themselves.

It would be premature to conclude that all random phenomena are simply the inconsequential off-shoots of deterministic processes that we do not fully understand or cannot accurately control. The unpredictability at the heart of matter and the unpredictability of human choice present formidable obstacles to such a sweeping conclusion. What is clear is that a vast range of phenomena, which we lump together under the umbrella of chance, can be adequately explained without the need to invoke pure chance.

Order out of chaos

Not only do deterministic processes yield observable phenomena which appear random, but random processes yield pattern and regularity when observed in the aggregate. So much so that it almost appears, over a wide range of experience, that randomness is a pre-condition of order. Children in primary schools, tossing coins, quickly see that though the outcome of the individual toss is highly uncertain, the proportion of heads in a large number of tosses is almost always close to a half. The sex ratio throughout the world has remained remarkably stable even though the sex of the individual child cannot yet be predicted. Life insurance companies are built on the fact that age specific death rates in a given society remain constant over reasonably long periods of time even though none of us can predict the death of any individual with certainty. Likewise it is possible to calculate the dose of radiation emitted by a radio-active isotope in spite of the uncertainty about when a particular atom will disintegrate. The gas laws – and many of the other laws of physics – are statistical in the sense that they describe the average effect of a large number of random movements of particles of one kind or another. Similar phenomena occur all the way from the atomic level, through the biological to the social. In fact it is at the social end of the scale that these regularities often occasion the most surprise. Although individuals may act freely and unpredictably, the aggregate effects of these many unrelated acts display remarkable regularities.

We noted in Chapter 1 that Adolphe Quetelet was so impressed by the similarity between the patterns found in social data and those dealt with by physics that he took over from Auguste Comte the term social physics to describe his social researches.[8] Though his belief in the possibility of a science of society on a par with physics seems naive in retrospect, the remarkable regularities which his tables revealed continue to fascinate us. Even today many people are just as puzzled as he was by what law of necessity constrains behaviour so that the number of suicides remains so nearly constant from year to year. Does it not call into question the idea of man's free will? If it had been decreed, for example, that so many suicides (give or take a few) 'must' occur in London in a year, does not that imply some constraint on an individual's supposed freedom to commit the act. If by November, say, the total was still far short of the quota would there not be a need for extra suicides so that the annual total might be reached? Prince Albert, a pupil of Quetelet, did not think so, and he was right.[9] The difficulty arises from confusing two senses of the word 'law' already noted; a confusion which is made harder to eradicate by speaking, as their contemporaries sometimes did, of social laws as the laws of God. They apparently thought of God as enacting social laws in the manner of parliaments. That is, by declaring that such and such shall be so and then using the appropriate law enforcement agencies to see that the laws are obeyed. Natural laws – including those relating to society – are not like this. They are descriptions of the way that things are, not prescriptions of the way they ought to be. The gas laws follow as a logical consequence of the random movement of the molecules – the molecules are not constrained in any way by the need to 'obey' the gas laws. Social laws are of exactly the same kind. They are descriptions of what people do with their freedom. There is no logical reason why the number of suicides should not double in one particular year but for this to happen there would have to be some basic change in individual attitudes or the social environment. Florence Nightingale saw enormous gains to be made in the betterment of the poor by these discoveries.[10] In so far as this involved seeing laws as something which could be relied on and used to work for the improvement of society, rather than a prison limiting individual freedom, she was right.[11]

If we go back to the sequences of pseudo-random numbers generated by a purely deterministic process the duality or complementarity of chance and law becomes apparent. For if we were to take a sufficiently long series of such numbers we would find that each of the digits 0, 1 up to 9 occurred with almost equal frequency and the extent of such deviations as did arise would almost certainly lie within limits which could be prescribed in advance. Determinism at one level thus generates randomness at the next level, which produces regularity at the next higher level of aggregation. It is therefore not at all obvious how far back this alternation might go if we were able to probe ever more deeply into the ultimate nature of matter – that is, which, of chance and order, is the more fundamental.

There are more subtle ways in which chance can lead to certainty. Earlier in the chapter we spoke of deterministic processes concerned with changes over time. We quoted results to the effect that a deterministic law of change could have unpredictable consequences. The converse is also true. A process whose law of development is a random one can have an entirely predictable outcome. Thus even though we may not be able to predict the short term future we can predict the terminal state. Put in another way; we know the destination even though we cannot predict the path by which it will be reached. Such processes have especial relevance when meeting Monod's point that randomness in a process rules out the possibility of purpose. Processes which develop in time, according to probabilistic, rather than deterministic, laws, are called stochastic processes. The word stochastic here is a synonym for random. The theory of stochastic processes is highly mathematical and it would be impracticable to use mathematical language and arguments here. However, such processes are so fundamental to an understanding of the role and possible purpose of chance in the scheme of things that some attempt to come to grips with the basic ideas is essential. Eigen and Winkler have done a great service in their book *The Laws of the Game*,[12] by constructing games played with beads and dice which exemplify many of the characteristics of stochastic processes. These are designed to imitate the random processes that go on in nature – competition among different species for food, for example – and so to demonstrate the sometimes surprising course which events take. Here we shall be much more modest by selecting a few processes which have parallels in most people's experience and which illustrate some vital points, albeit in a highly simplified fashion.

Let us start with a simple epidemic process. Assume a closed population of people (or animals) who are all susceptible to a new virus which is introduced into the population. If all people mix freely the virus will spread from one to another. A number of questions now arise to which the answers are, perhaps, not immediately obvious. Will all the people eventually contract the disease and, if not, how many can we expect to succumb? How long will it take? What will be the pattern of growth of the epidemic? The answer to all these questions is, of course, 'it all depends'. It depends on how frequently people meet, how long it is before an infected person can infect another and so on. The theory of epidemics examines such processes by making probabilistic assumptions about the rate and manner of contact, among other things. The simplest such assumption is known as homogeneous mixing, which means that any pair of individuals are equally likely to make contact in a small interval of time as any other, and that all individuals behave independently. Under these circumstances it can be shown that it is certain that the epidemic will continue until everyone has been infected. In that sense the outcome is certain and it can be predicted before the process starts. What cannot be predicted is the order in which individuals will succumb. Thus if we were to imagine a list of names arranged in order of infection, all permutations would be equally likely. The stage of the epidemic at which any named individual would contract the disease would be quite unpredictable. If one were cast in the role of a malevolent deity with the desire to infect a whole population, there would therefore be no need to plan the course of the epidemic in detail. If the sole object was to see that everyone was infected, it would be quite sufficient to introduce the virus and then leave its spread to 'chance'. Nothing that mattered would be gained by interfering at the detailed level of who infects whom.

Similar models are used to describe the spread of rumours in a human population, or of innovations among, say farmers. If one can rely on the individuals mixing freely the 'news will get around' without the need to prescribe the path which it will follow.

This process is a very simple example of a stochastic process with a predictable outcome. There are many more. In another type of epidemic model a new feature is introduced which limits the number of contacts each person can make. Suppose, in a rumour-mongering situation, each person who hears the rumour passes it on to exactly two other people. On the assumption of homogeneous mixing, it will no longer be true, in general, that everyone will hear. The number will vary, of course, but on average it will be 80% of the population. Which 80% is not predictable but, in aggregate terms, the outcome is certain.[13]

A somewhat different way in which order results from the chaotic behaviour of a stochastic process is in what is known as 'steady state' behaviour. Again we take an example, this time from marketing. Suppose a number of different brands of some commodity are available to consumers and that all are virtually equivalent as far as their efficacy is concerned. Individual consumers may switch from one brand to another in a haphazard fashion so that the pattern of purchases for any person is not predictable. What the manufacturers of each brand wish to know is what share of the market they can expect to obtain. Once again the answer to such questions depends upon the precise way in which the sequence of individual purchases is made. One of the simplest models is what is known as a Markov chain. Such models have not been as successful in this field as in some others but that does not affect the point we wish to make. We imagine that each person behaves as if they selected their next purchase by lot. However, the chances in the lottery are allowed to depend on the most recent purchase. Thus, the chance of buying brand P, given that the last brand bought was H, need not be the same as if the last brand was J. People's preferences are thus allowed to depend in a simple way upon their present experience (but not upon their previous purchasing history). It is quite easy to simulate such a process by throwing dice to determine the next purchase in the sequence. The result will be a sequence of different brands with no clear pattern. If, however, we aggregate the results for a large number of purchasers a pattern will begin to emerge as time passes. The proportions buying each brand will begin to stabilize so that each manufacturer has a fixed (but usually unequal) share of the market. The surprising thing to the uninitiated is that these steady state shares are entirely unrelated to the initial shares. Thus, with such a simple model there is no long-term advantage in getting in first and taking a large initial share. This will quickly be eroded and the final shares will depend solely on the probabilities governing change. For the same reason no re-allocation of shares by outside edict can have a lasting effect unless the switching probabilities are also changed.

Such processes are very common. Voting behaviour, social mobility, labour mobility, health care, are only some of the fields where such models have been applied. In all of them the development of the process proceeds in a random fashion which in a local sense makes it highly unpredictable. Yet overall the aggregate effect is certainly predictable.

This phenomenon is so widespread that whenever stabilities occur in nature or society it is quite likely to be the result of a stochastic process having reached its steady state. The remarkable persistence of the form of income distribution and social structure over time may well, in part at least, be explicable in such terms. One of the most celebrated examples is known as Zipf's law. George Zipf wrote a remarkable book, entitled *Human Behavior and the Principle of Least Effort*,[14] in which he aimed to show that many social (and other) regularities could be explained as consequences of this basic principle which he supposed to underlly human behaviour. One of the 'laws' which he discussed concerned the relation between rank and size of cities, firms and such like. For example, if, say the steel producers of the United States are listed in order of size (measured by output) then we discover the remarkable fact that the product of the size and the rank order is nearly constant. Many attempts have been made to explain this phenomenon. The most convincing are those which treat changes in size over time as a stochastic process, and which then show that the steady state has the form required by Zipf's law.

All of these examples illustrate the way in which a process, developing randomly in time, can exhibit regularities which are, in a sense, inherent in the laws of change themselves. In other words, order is a consequence of chaos. Such processes are more complicated than the simplest examples we used concerning the birth ratio and such like. With them we were concerned with a large number of independent events. The latter processes involve a degree of dependence in that what happens next depends on the current state. The unpredictable strands woven by the processes at the individual level thus combine to produce a predictable and stable pattern.

It would be misleading to suggest that all stochastic processes have a single outcome which can be predicted with certainty in advance. Often there will be a number of terminal states, and which one is reached may depend critically on the random behaviour in the early stages of the process. For example, if we generalize our simple epidemic model by supposing that each individual, once infected, is removed from the population after a random length of time, then two quite different outcomes may be possible. If the infection is introduced by a single individual and if he is withdrawn before making contact with anyone else then, clearly, there will be no epidemic. On the other hand if he succeeds in infecting several others before being withdrawn the chances of an epidemic building up are much greater. Whether or not the epidemic does take hold depends, in a critical fashion, on how many contacts an individual can expect to make during the time he is active in the population. If, on average, this is less than one in a large population, it is virtually certain there will be no epidemic. If it exceeds one, there is a reasonable chance that the epidemic will spread to a large proportion of the population. Thus if, on average, each person contacts two people while actively infectious, there is an even chance that the epidemic will develop. Whether or not it does so on any particular occasion depends very much on the chance contacts which occur in the very early stages. The situation is not unlike that occurring when a spark falls into a tinder dry forest. Whether a fire will start depends on how much wood or leaves are ignited before the original spark is extinguished. Once the fire has taken hold it is liable to spread rapidly. Such processes are characterized by what is termed a threshold such that a very small variation in the initial conditions around the threshold value is sufficient to lead to widely different terminal states.

If the processes involved in evolution were of this kind it might appear that chance again has a determining role in deciding what direction development takes. Suppose such a threshold phenomenon occurred at a vital juncture in the line of development leading to human life then it would appear that life might not have developed, and the fact that it did can only be put down to chance. This argument depends on two assumptions both of which are highly questionable. One is that the 'initial' conditions were near the threshold so that the outcome was so finely balanced that a chance 'puff of wind' would be sufficient to turn the outcome one way or the other. If the threshold were clearly exceeded, the outcome would have been virtually certain and this would seem the more likely alternative. The second assumption is that the situation concerned is unique. If a somewhat similar set of circumstances were to appear many times, then a successful outcome on at least one of them would be highly probable.

In fact, it is commonly the case that the number of terminal states of a system may be quite small in relation to the vast number of possible paths by which they may be reached. Even if only one of them is favourable to some desired outcome, a sufficient number of repetitions will ensure that that particular outcome occurs sooner or later.

A somewhat different kind of stochastic model has been used by Kauffman[15] to study the role of chance in the construction of contemporary organisms. The degree of order and stability which they display would, one might suppose, require a great deal of prior planning or, alternatively, a long period of intense natural selection in order to eliminate those structures not having the requisite degree of metabolic stability. Kauffman investigated the alternative hypothesis that contemporary organisms are randomly constructed molecular automata. He did this by considering a large collection of genes which are postulated to be in one of two states – on or off. The genes are randomly connected and the state of any gene at one time, T say, is assumed to be determined by the states of those genes at time $T-1$ to which it is directly linked. Chance enters the process in two ways: first in the network of connections, and secondly in the function which determines what state any gene is in in terms of the states of those with which it is connected. This function can be thought of as a table from which we read off the state of a gene at time T from the stages at $T-1$ of those connected to it. From all such tables which could possibly exist the one in use is supposed to have been selected at random. Once the network and the table have been fixed the succession of states through which the system moves is completely determined.

It turns out that biologically plausible behaviour is only possible if each gene is affected by just two or three other genes. In a network of a few hundred binary genes there are millions upon millions of possible states in which the whole system can be. One might then expect that the system would wend its way through a very large number of states and so exhibit no sign of stability. Rather surprisingly the opposite is true. Wherever the system starts it will enter a closed loop of states through which it will continue to cycle. The length of such a cycle is likely to be very short, perhaps only five or ten states, so that the system is highly stable. Even if a further element of randomness is introduced by allowing one of the states at T–1 to be mis-read, the conclusion is not seriously affected. The system will now occasionally move to a new cycle, but it is very probable that it will return to its original path.

Kauffman goes on to show that such models successfully predict a variety of features of living organisms such as cell replication time or the differentiation of a cell from one mode of behaviour to a relatively small set of alternative modes. He concludes his paper with the remark: 'Large, randomly assembled nets of binary elements behave with simplicity, stability, and order. It seems unlikely that Nature has made no use of such probable and reliable systems, both to initiate evolution and protect its progeny.'[16] One might go further and add that since such a degree of order is almost inevitable, Nature could hardly avoid using it.

This necessarily rather abstract attempt to describe some elementary stochastic processes does not pretend to more than hint at the mechanism of evolutionary development. Its sole purpose is to emphasize that even very simple and artificial random processes can be quite subtle, and that the inter-relation of chance and certainty needs careful investigation. We leave this part of our discussion with an example of a further type of behaviour which adds another twist to the chance and certainty spiral. This concerns what may be called a quasi-steady state. One example arises by making a small alteration to the epidemic with withdrawals. Instead of infectious individuals being removed from the population, after random lengths of time they are returned to the pool of susceptibles and so may become infected again. Such a process will typically continue for a very long time but sooner or later it will cease with no one remaining infectious at all. However, provided that the epidemic survives extinction in the early stages, the time before it finally ceases will be very long indeed. For most of that period it will be in a state where a roughly constant proportion (possibly quite large) of the population will be infected. This quasi-steady state may be much more relevant for practical purposes since it may well be that the final state is not reached before other circumstances intervene. A rather simpler example illustrates this point and it is quite easy to construct a simple game which the reader may play by him or herself. We need a spinner with 10 sides, or any other means of selecting one of the numbers 1, 2, 3, . . . , 10 at random. (Readers with access to tables of random numbers or home computers will find these much the simplest way to generate the numbers required.) We proceed as follows.

(a) Draw 10 random digits and count how many of them are between 1 and 5, both inclusive. This number is called the current score. (It can clearly vary between 0 and 10.)

(b) Draw 10 more random digits and count how many of them are between 1 and the current score, both inclusive. This number becomes the new current score.

(c) The procedure is repeated until the current score first reaches 0 or 10. (If the game were continued beyond this point the score would be unchanged at either 0 or 10 indefinitely.)

At the first step 5 is the most likely outcome and if this occurs the most likely outcome is also 5 and so on. One might guess, therefore that a succession of 5s was the most probable sequence. However, there will always be the chance of an unlucky run where the score sinks to zero or rises to ten. In fact, it may be shown that this is certain to happen sooner or later. This rather imprecise reasoning suggests that there might be two characteristic modes of behaviour for this stochastic process. One would consist of a sequence of fairly constant values in the neighbourhood of 5, followed, sooner or later, by a drift to 0 or 10. This is, in fact, something like what often occurs. The following is a fairly typical sequence of scores obtained in actual play of the game:

5 6 6 5 6 9 9 7 4 5 4 4 3 3 4 5 3 0 .

First there is the quasi-stationary behaviour with values near 5, then termination at the upper boundary is almost reached followed by another quasi-stationary phase with final termination at zero. The reader is invited to try some experiments to confirm that this is a fairly normal kind of outcome.

Although it requires much more patience, a more convincing illustration of the point being made can be had by selecting from the digits 1, 2, . . . 100. Then the sequence will typically hover around the 50 for a considerable time before drifting away. In fact the larger the number of digits the longer will this quasi-stationary behaviour tend to continue. Two things about this process which are certain are first, that the score will eventually reach either 0 or 100 (or whatever the largest digit is) and, secondly, that for an initial period the score is likely to remain approximately constant.

Although they are immensely more complicated, there is a distinct similarity between this game and some of the processes describing chemical reactions discussed by Nicolis and Prigogine.[17] It serves as a further illustration that the aggregate effects of highly random processes may exhibit regularities of different kinds in areas where intuition is an uncertain guide.

None of the processes discussed here should be regarded as more than 'toys' for those beginning to gain some inkling of what is implied by saying that all of experience is a stochastic process. However, toys are not merely playthings to while away the time, but instruments by which we acquire experience of, and insight into, the working of the world. The reader whose appetite has been whetted by our simple example will now be ready to cut his teeth on the more elaborate and realistic games of Eigen and Winkler.[18] At the very least we should have convinced the reader that the mere existence of chance processes in nature is not a sufficient ground for inferring the absence of purpose.

Not only are real life stochastic processes more complicated, but they also interact with one another. The amount of food available in a particular habitat will depend on many uncertain factors of which the weather will be among the chief. Similarly, the size of an animal population will depend on many other uncertain factors. But each process will affect the other. The more animals, the more food will be eaten and, perhaps, the less seed will ripen for the next year's crop. The fewer animals, the more food for each, and so, perhaps, more and healthier offspring to compete for next year's food crop, and so on. One stochastic process thus forms part of the environment in which others operate and so affects which of the possible options open to them will, in fact, be taken. Anything approaching a realistic attempt to model this level of complexity in a fully comprehensive fashion seems a long way off. This fact should make us very cautious about coming to a conclusion as to whether chance or certainty comes out on top in the end.

A thought which will be developed later is that only in a world with a sufficient degree of randomness is there enough flexibility to combine a broadly determined line of development with adequate room for the exercise of real freedom on the part of individuals.

We conclude this chapter by noting that we, ourselves 'use' chance to bring about our desired ends because it is often more 'efficient' to do so. The obvious implication that what we find advantageous may be merely a reflection of what God has been doing all along is brought out in the following chapter.

The use of chance

We naturally think of chance as something to which we are subject. It is not so often recognized that we sometimes create and use chance events to further our own purposes. Some of these uses are very simple, others are highly sophisticated. Sometimes we use chance to achieve a particular end, and sometimes, as a deliberate attempt to eliminate any influence our wishes might have on the outcome. One of the most common and familiar uses of chance is to make a fair decision on who shall take the first turn in a game like snooker, or who shall resign from a committee. The aim is to eliminate any bias on the part of the decision maker. If all eligible contestants or candidates have an equal chance of being chosen, then the method embodies an obvious principle of fairness. This is not necessarily the only way of being fair to all parties and it is instructive to consider why we often prefer to toss a coin rather than rely on some deterministic method. For example, if two teams are to play a series of games against each other they could take turns in starting. Each would then have an equal share of whatever advantage there is to be gained from making the first move. If, instead of doing this, we toss a coin each time, we retain the property of having each team starting on an equal number of occasions in the long run but, in addition, we introduce an element of surprise which adds interest for the spectator and helps to keep the players on their toes. By eliminating an element of monotony from the series the quality of the contest is enhanced without placing either team at a disadvantage.

Randomization, as it is called, is not only used to decide who takes first turn in a game but it forms an integral part of many. The outcome of some games, of course, depends only on chance, through the roll of a die or shuffling of cards. These have a certain appeal, especially when the players are of unequal ability, but their interest quickly begins to pall. Much more interesting are those games which are a mixture of skill and chance. Bridge and many such card games are good examples. The cards are dealt at random but thereafter the result depends on the skill of the players. Chance here serves several purposes. It embodies the principle of fairness by ensuring that players have no long term advantage in the dealing of the cards. Secondly, it allows the weaker players to win occasionally when the deal turns out particularly favourable to them. Skill will count in the long run but the short term upsets enliven the game and provide some reward for the less skilful players. Thirdly, and more important, it tests the skill of the players by continually presenting them with new situations which they have never encountered before. It would, of course, be possible for the governing body of the game to issue a catalogue of possible deals calculated to offer the players a variety of challenges. Apart from the practical difficulty of ensuring that players did not look at the catalogue beforehand, such a method would be enormously costly and offer little in return. Chance can be relied on to generate the requisite variety with far less bother. In the long run it achieves the maximum of variety and challenge with the minimum of effort. In this sense leaving the dealing to chance is much more efficient than trying to engineer all the details of the hands to be played in advance.

Chance is also used as a means of protecting an individual, a firm, or other body against uncertainty. This somewhat paradoxical statement can be illustrated from two fields in which it is widely used by statisticians. These illustrate how chance can, in a manner of speaking, be used to neutralize uncertainty and so attain a determinate end. The first example comes from the theory of games. The use of the term 'game' here is somewhat misleading. Although it certainly covers games in the ordinary sense of the word it refers, more generally, to contests of any kind between opposing parties (often two) in which each tries to outwit the other. Two armies in battle or several firms competing for a market are examples of games in this extended sense. Such a game is characterized by the fact that each party has open to them a number of choices. Any combination of choices will lead to a 'pay-off' to each of them. A central feature of such a game is that the individual decisions have to be made without full knowledge of what the opponents are going to do. The theory of games is concerned with how to find good strategies for winning games. Uncertainty arises because of the imperfect information available to the contestants about their opponents' intentions. To see how chance can be used to counter this situation we consider a very simple game played between two players A and B. A coin is to be tossed and each player must predict how it will fall. If A and B make the same prediction, B pays A a pound. If they differ, A pays B the same amount. (Note that the actual outcome of the toss does not affect the pay-off.) The game proceeds indefinitely in this fashion. Suppose that A decides on a formula which will tell him what to call on any occasion. After a time B, who has studied A's sequence of choices, may be able to determine what the formula is. Once he has done this he can predict what A is going to call and so he can call the opposite and so guarantee himself a pound each time. However, A, who is just as intelligent as B, can see that whatever plan he adopts there is the risk that B will be able to deduce what it is and so take advantage of his knowledge to A's downfall. Even if B cannot predict exactly what A is going to call he may, nevertheless, learn enough to be right more often than not. What is A to do to protect himself from B's powers of prediction? He must obviously ensure that his past behaviour provides no clues about what he is going to do next. The only way A can be certain of concealing his intentions from B is not to know, himself, what he is going to do next! He can achieve this by making his choice at random. Suppose, therefore, he decides to toss a coin and call whatever falls uppermost. Whatever B chooses A can now be certain that, in the long run, his net winnings cannot fall below zero. This may seem a modest enough achievement, but with any non-random strategy there is a real risk of a steadily growing loss. A's randomized strategy thus neutralizes any ability that B may have to predict A's behaviour and this protects him from serious loss. Notice that A does not need to conceal from B that he is making choices at random. The coin can be tossed in full public view without B being in any better position.

Many decision making situations are often described as being games against nature. To speak of 'nature' as an opponent may seem a little far-fetched but it is a useful fiction. We cannot now argue as we did above because, unless we believe that 'nature' is a malevolent deity seeking to outwit us, we cannot attribute the power to reason about our behaviour to nature. Statisticians often view the choices made in designing an experiment or selecting a sample as games against nature.

Let us imagine that a psychologist wishes to test the efficacy of a new method of teaching reading. To do this she proposes to obtain two groups of children of similar age and background. One group will be taught by a traditional method and the other by the new. It clearly will not do to take one group from one school and one from another and use these for the experiment. It may be that different styles of teaching already in use in these schools will have affected the way the children will respond in the experiment. If the new method then comes out superior we shall not know whether to attribute the result to the new method or to other school-related factors. Past educational background, different IQ levels or parental attitudes might all have contributed to the observed difference. In anticipation of such criticism our experimenter realizes that she will somehow have to 'mix up' the children in some way so that any such undetected group differences will be neutralized. She might recognize that factors such as age, sex, IQ and so on might confound the issue and so seek to balance these out in forming the two groups that the experiment requires. But how could she be sure that there was no other crucial factor which might be concentrated in one group in sufficient strength to mask the real effect of the new teaching method?

The experimenter can be thought of as playing a 'game' against 'nature'. She is trying to make the two groups as alike as possible whereas the fictitious opponent is trying to do the opposite. The choices open to the experimenter consist of all the possible ways of dividing the children up into two equal groups. Only by choosing the allocation purely at random can she safeguard herself against a hidden bias. It is important to be clear about the precise nature of this protection. There can be no guarantee that *in this particular experiment* there will be no such bias. It is always possible that the children with the greatest aptitude will, by chance, be allocated to one group or the other. What the randomization does ensure is that the chance of this happening will be very small. This means that in a large number of experiments of this kind the great majority will be based on fairly matched groups. As a principle of scientific conduct, therefore, it ensures that very few experiments will be spoilt by having grossly unbalanced experimental groups. In this sense the experimenter is protected against being caught out by nature.

A similar principle applies in sample surveys where information about a large population is obtained by examining a relatively small number of its members. Market researchers could not possibly question all potential customers about their tastes, habits and purchasing intentions. Opinion pollsters cannot afford to interview more than a few hundred or thousand people. Medical researchers could not, even if they wished, try out a new drug on all people for whom it might be beneficial. The quality testing of light bulbs or ammunition is destructive and examining every single item would leave none for use. In the sciences, limits on time and money prevent the experimental scientist from making as many measurements as he could wish. Progress in all these fields of investigation is only possible if we can ensure that the samples, which have to serve as a substitute for the whole, are representative. To some this seems impossible. Malcolm Muggeridge was speaking for many when he claimed that it was absurd to suppose that one could find out what millions thought by questioning a few hundred. That he was wrong is a consequence of sampling theory – among the greatest achievments of modern statistics. One can, in fact, learn almost as much about a population of 40 million from a sample of 2000 as about a population of 40 thousand – provided that the sample is properly chosen. Again we have a game against nature. The sampler is faced with choosing which of the enormous number of possible samples he will actually use. How should he select the sample so as to protect himself against getting an unrepresentative – and hence misleading – sample? Once more the answer lies in randomization or resorting to chance. If a method of drawing the sample can be contrived which gives each possible sample a known probability of being drawn, then all is well, in the long run at least. It is always possible that an occasional 'bad' sample will occur, but the chance of this happening is small and hence, in the long run, few such will occur. Random sampling in some form or other is actually much better than subjective selection and the user can never be justly accused of allowing his own prejudices to influence the outcome of his enquiry. The only proper answer to the question 'why pick on me?' from someone selected by such a sampling process is 'for no reason at all'.

We have already noted the role of chance in contributing to the interest of a game when used to decide who goes first. Of course it plays a much more important role as the game develops. Most games derive much of their spice from just the right blend of chance and skill. A novice darts or snooker player will derive little satisfaction from the game if he can rarely score a double or only pot a ball by accident. But there is little excitement at the other extreme either where skill is supreme, because then the course of the game is predictable and therefore monotonous. Billiards played by an expert is somewhat like this and when such a situation arises, the rules have to be changed if the game is to survive. Many of the best ball games like tennis, cricket and snooker rely for their appeal on the fact that even the best players cannot precisely control their moves and so new and unexpected situations are continually arising. There is just enough uncertainty arising from environmental conditions or limitation of the skill of the player to maintain interest and excitement. The role of chance here is to make the game more challenging by testing the player's resourcefulness and skill in dealing with new situations. In some games the use of chance goes further. It may be injected deliberately to mislead the opponent and so take advantage of him. The bridge player may bluff, or the tennis player may deliberately play a weak shot which so surprises the opponent that he is caught off balance and so makes an error.

The fact that large aggregates of random phenomena exhibit regularities makes it possible to create regularity out of randomness. As every amateur decorator knows the aim when painting a large flat area is to get as smooth a finish as possible. This involves applying just the right amount of paint as evenly as possible. With care and practice this can be done with a brush. However, a much better job can be done with a spray. This breaks the paint up into tiny droplets and projects them more or less at random over the surface. A very short burst would produce an irregular, speckled effect, but a more prolonged exposure produces a very even covering. The reason is that the number of drops per unit area will show a very small relative variation if that number is very large. The same effect could be achieved if it were possible to devise a machine that would deliver exactly the same number of droplets to each square centimetre. However, this would be enormously costly and the effect would not be noticeably different from the random scattering achieved by the spray gun. There are other, rather similar situations, where a cheap and quick random scattering is more efficient than a precise spacing. Sowing seed in a drill is one such example. To ensure equal spacing of the seedlings it would be necessary to space the seeds at equal intervals along the drill (and even then some would not germinate). However, it is much easier to scatter the seeds haphazardly at about the right density and then to thin them out at a later stage. Even if it were possible to achieve the exact spacing of seed there would be little, if any, advantage in doing so.

Our final example, showing how chance may be harnessed to some useful end, is rather specialized but instructive nevertheless. Suppose we wish to find the area of the following figure.

It might represent an island or the area of land above a certain height. There is clearly no simple formula depending on a few easily measured dimensions as there is with rectangles and circles. One method would be to cover the figure with a transparent fine grid and count the number of squares inside the figure. Imagine now a three-dimensional figure of highly irregular form. A similar method could, in principle, be used but it would be very tedious. A much simpler method is to enclose the figure in a circle or square (a sphere or cube in three dimensions). Points are then chosen at random within the regular figure or solid. This can easily be done using random numbers for the co-ordinates. As the number of points increases the proportion which fall in the figure will approach its relative area. By making the number of points large enough, the area can be estimated to any desired degree of accuracy.

Far from being the antithesis of order, purpose and design, chance can be used to good effect as these examples show. Even where its use is not strictly necessary there may well be benefits in allowing it a place. Chance ensures fairness; it provides protection and ensures validity in sampling and design of experiments; it adds interest, excitement and challenge in games and often provides a simple and efficient way of carrying out difficult tasks. The science of chance, born in the sixteenth and seventeenth centuries and developed to a high degree in the twentieth, has proved to be a powerful tool. It not only helps us to understand the complicated natural processes by which we are surrounded, but can be used to achieve ends which would otherwise be beyond our reach. As Kauffman[19] speculated, it would not be surprising to find that chance played an analogous role on the grand scale before we came on the scene.

5

God of Chance

The approach

The time has come to consider whether or not chance can be accommodated within a theistic framework and, if so, how. The conclusion reached is liable to be strongly influenced by the point of departure. We must therefore be clear about the options available and our reasons for making a choice among them. Broadly speaking there appear to be three ways open to us. One is to give priority to revelation as found in the Bible or tradition. A second is to take science as definitive and the third is to attempt to give equal weight to each.

The first is exemplified by those who take their stand on the literal truth of the Bible. Such a course admits of many variations depending on the sophistication of one's approach to biblical interpretation but in all forms the Bible is the arbiter of what is true. In so far as scientific discoveries appear to contradict the Bible, they must be rejected. As we shall see, it is far from clear that the Bible speaks with one voice on the matter of chance, but there is no doubt that most of those who adopt this position have supposed it to deny that there is any such thing as pure chance. Chance is then merely a reflection of our ignorance.

The way which attempts to grant equal validity to the Bible and to science is exemplified by Pollard in his *Chance and Providence*.[1] Speaking as a scientist and a theologian and moving easily within both spheres of knowledge he felt that neither could be lightly dismissed. Both spheres commanded his loyalty and respect and his task was to harmonize the truths of each in a way which did justice to both.

The remaining option is to begin with science and then to seek to interpret biblical truth in the light of scientific knowledge. To those who see the issue in adversarial terms this will seem like asking the theologian to fight with one hand tied behind his back. This approach will also draw the reproach of those who see it as abandoning the sure foundation of divine truth for the shifting sands of what can never be more than the provisional and incomplete theories fashioned by fallible minds. Nevertheless, it has much to commend it. The cynic will observe that such a strategy would have served well in the past. The entrenched positions of biblical fundamentalism have been abandoned one by one. Even among conservative biblical scholars views on the manner and date of creation (witness the *New Bible Dictionary*[2]) have bent to the scientific wind to a degree which would have alarmed their predecessors. Even though the tentative, and occasionally arrogant, claims of scientists have sometimes had to be abandoned this does not alter the fact that our present world view is based on a solid foundation of empirical knowledge accepted by the community of scientists. New paradigms and revolutionary discoveries do not usually contradict what is already known. Einstein did not show that Newton's mechanics was wrong but, rather, he set it in a larger context which showed clearly the limits of its validity. It is unthinkable that future discoveries should take us back to the world view of the ancients and show that 'the Bible was right after all'.

But there are better reasons for adopting this approach. We start from the position that all truth is God's truth. Furthermore the truth which comes through scientific endeavour is, in a sense, simpler and more easily recognized for what it is than are the more subtle and elusive truths of the spirit. Thus, in making science our starting point we are not according it a higher status than revealed truth – quite the contrary. Scientific truth is concerned with the elemental facts about the construction of the physical universe in which the divine drama is played out. It hardly touches the deeper and more ultimate things like divine love with all that that entails. Because it is concerned primarily with things we can measure and weigh, scientific truth can be expressed in clearer, less ambiguous terms on which it is easier to reach a consensus. On the contrary it is notoriously difficult to capture the elusive and profound mysteries of God in forms of words or, indeed, any other symbolism.

In simple terms we are saying: let us accept the truths about the physical universe which our God-given minds show us through science and then we shall be better placed to make sense of the more profound truths with which the Christian revelation is primarily concerned. We claim that the person who takes science seriously is better placed to comprehend the higher truths than one who tenaciously clings to out-moded thought forms about matters which, after all, are only secondary. History is on the side of this argument. Few would deny that we have a fuller and richer understanding of the

greatness of God today than our forbears did. This is almost entirely
due to the discovery that we live in a larger, more complex and more
exciting cosmos than could have been dreamed of in the middle ages.
Much controversy and heartache, not to mention persecution, would
have been avoided had this view of things been taken more often in the
past.

To adopt such an open attitude to truth is, of course, risky, as these
things are commonly judged. It requires a willingness to leave the
apparently secure foothold we already have, without knowing
whether or when we shall find firm ground again. Nevertheless, faith
and honesty require nothing less. It is no use following the example of
the two ladies (doubtless apocryphal) who prayed 'O, God grant that
this evolution be not true but if it is give us grace to hush it up'. No one
who heeds the story of Abraham can suppose that faith requires us to
stay at home in familiar surroundings.

At the risk of undue repetition, let us put the point another way. In
taking the facts of science as our starting point we are not setting up
the works of man in judgment on the word of God. Rather we are
using the light which God gives us in science to illuminate the word of
God so that its real meaning becomes clearer.

In the following section we shall attempt the beginnings of a natural
theology which takes chance seriously. Then we shall move on to
consider what the Bible in its Old and New Testaments has to say and
how this may be interpreted in the light of the scientific story. Then,
since revealed truth has to be interpreted and expressed in the life of
the church, we shall look at how those steeped in the Bible have acted
in the light of what they found there. Only then, and after dismissing
some extra-theological considerations, shall we be in a position to see
what the theological map begins to look like in the post-Monod era.
The emphasis in this chapter is mainly concerned with the doctrine of
creation – with the role that chance plays in the grand scheme of
things. Even if this question can be satisfactorily resolved it raises
another, and for the Christian, a more serious issue. This concerns
God's Providence. How in a world of chance can we conceive of God's
activity? This is the theme of the next chapter on Chance and
Providence.

A natural theology of chance

Natural theology is out of favour. The idea that we can make valid
inferences about the nature and purpose of God from his work in
creation is so fraught with hazards that it has largely been abandoned.
Our aim here is much more modest. The question we seek to answer

is: 'If the scientific picture of the role of chance in evolution at all levels
is a true one, does this leave room for God and, if so, what view of his
nature is consistent with our scientific knowledge?'

The answer to this question will clearly depend on how we regard
the nature of chance. In earlier chapters we have noted that scientists
themselves hold varying views so there can be no agreed scientific
view. Among physicists there have been three main responses to the
uncertainty at the quantum level which have been summarized by
Barbour.[3] The first is that chance is a reflection of human ignorance.
Einstein, Planck, de Broglie and Bohm are named as among the
minority of physicists who have taken this view. All, in various ways,
believed that it would be ultimately possible to construct a theory of
matter in which all uncertainty is removed. MacKay's[4] response to
Monod was essentially of this kind as, from the opposite view, was
that of Schoffeniels.[5] As we have already noted, this interpretation is
congenial to those who set high value on the sovereignty of God. It
does not, of course, imply that there must be a God, only that if there
is one then he must be responsible for all that happens at least as far as
the 'mechanics' of the universe is concerned. In solving one problem it
raises another. By espousing determinism it makes it difficult to see
how human freedom can be real. Without wishing to deny that a
theology can be constructed from this premise, it will be clear from
the tendency of the preceding chapters that our sympathies lie
elsewhere.

The second scientific view of chance is agnostic in that it says we
cannot know whether what we have called pure chance exists. This
may be ascribed either to the limitations on experimental method or
our conceptual abilities. Either way we must simply accept the fact
that there can be no answer to the question whether there is an
irreducible element of chance in the creation. Although this may
appear theologically neutral, it poses the theologian with an almost
impossible task. He must construct his theology so as to be capable of
accommodating either view. It is true that he can adopt a deterministic or random philosophy without fear of what science can do to it, but
there must always be the doubt as to whether he is on the wrong track.

The third view in Barbour's list, associated with Heisenberg, is that
there is a fundamental indeterminacy in nature which no amount of
further knowledge can eradicate. We have argued that this is not
simply to be seen at the sub-atomic level, but is something which
pervades all levels of creation. The conclusion of our last chapter was
that whether or not there was such a thing as pure chance in any
ultimate sense was not the main issue. The fact of the matter is that the
practical effect is the same. Our contention is that if science is to be

taken seriously then chance must be regarded as an essential ingredient of the cosmos and the theologian must try to account for its presence and purpose.

With MacKay[6] we must strenuously resist the temptation to personify chance and so to think of it as a separate agent. In naming their gods the Greeks and Romans were at least explicit. Whether Tyche or Fortuna were on 'our side' or against us their supposed existence removed the need for further explanation. We shall therefore have no truck with solutions which regard chance as an entity alongside or opposed to God or any other gods. If a God worthy of the name exists, chance happenings must be his responsibility in some sense. If not, chance is simply part of the inexplicable nature of things.

Our basic position is therefore that chance is real and not wholly the product of our own ignorance; that chance happenings are part of God's overall plan but that events occur which do not express his direct intentions. Further, some events, for example, those resulting from free human decisions, may be contrary to that will.

It will be well to state explicitly the criteria which need to be satisfied by any account which aims to create a synthesis of the scientific and biblical points of view.

(i) It must take the facts of nature in their most obvious and natural sense. In particular it must treat chance as real and fundamental.

(ii) It must be capable of making sense of scripture and, in particular, it must not diminish God by assigning to him attributes which limit his power or compromise his nature revealed as love.

There are some questions which we may leave open. For example, whether God foresees all the consequences of the randomness in nature. We can allow that he is capable of doing so but this does not necessarily imply that he needs to do so. It is what he can do about it that matters.

We begin by questioning an assumption which constantly recurs when these issues are discussed. Roughly speaking, it is that order is evidence for a purposive God and chaos is evidence against. Meynell[7] made this point in his response to Monod, but it is clearly put by F. R. Tennant in his *Philosophical Theology* quoted by John Hick. He says:

> . . . the world is more or less intelligible, in that it happens to be more or less of a cosmos, when conceivably it might have been a self-subsistent and determinate 'chaos' in which similar events never occurred, none recurred, universals had no place, relations no fixity, things no nexus of determination and 'real' categories no foothold.[8]

Tennant goes on to say that the fact of order does not imply purposive intentions; we know that order does arise from such intentions but we do not know whether it is possible in their absence. However, the point we wish to challenge is whether it *is* conceivable that the cosmos might have been a self-subsistent and determinate chaos. If our analysis of chance is on the right lines then chaos and order are complementary; the presence of one seems to imply the other. Thus if we imagine a god setting out to create total chaos then surely the laws of large numbers would still apply and hence regularities on the large scale would be the inevitable concomitant of the primal chaos. Equally, at a higher level of aggregation still the interaction of these regularities might be expected to spark off a new generation of accidental happenings. It is not implausible to argue that whatever the nature of the most elemental happenings there will be, inevitably, a hierarchy of order and chaos in the resulting cosmos. Any argument for the existence of God on these lines thus founders.

For the same reason it is equally doubtful whether a wholly deterministic universe is conceivable at a level of complexity sufficient to support intelligent life. Purely deterministic machines are, of course, possible – we make them ourselves – but it may well be that in any highly complex deterministic world it may be impossible to have all the desired properties without so many 'accidental' happenings occurring as to create a measure of chaos. Computers do exactly what they are told but when programmes reach a certain level of complexity they seem to take on a life of their own, a fact which even the home computer enthusiast will have experienced.

This, of course, is speculation but bridled by the insights of the last chapter. But, if it is anywhere near the truth, it means that law and chance, order and chaos are not so much things to be justified or explained. They are simply the inevitable consequences of there being anything at all on a sufficiently large scale to support intelligent life. Even if there is a flaw in these arguments so that God had a real choice in the matter and could have excluded pure chance had he so wished, there may well have been positive reasons for incorporating chance into the creation on the grounds that the benefits outweighed the drawbacks.

For these reasons, as well as those set out in Chapter 3, I do not think that the presence (or absence) of chance in a cosmos tells us anything about the existence of God. All that we can hope to do is to deduce something about his nature from the kind of world we find ourselves in. In particular with whether the existing state of affairs is the expression of his intentions or whether it is outside his control or interest. This is the primary question since there would be little point in our concerning ourselves with a God who was not concerned with us.

The idea that chance has a place within the purpose of God is not a new one though it does not seem to have been fully developed. The weight of theological opinion, St Thomas Aquinas and his heirs excepted, seems to have regarded chance as the enemy of true religion and, largely, been intent on denying its existence. Even where the opposite seems to be the case further investigation shows otherwise. In the seventeenth century Sir Thomas Browne, with remarkable prescience, summed up the essence of the position being developed here when, in his *Religio Medici* he wrote, 'Those that hold that all things are governed by Fortune, had not erred had they not persisted there. . .'.[9] Unfortunately it is clear from the context of his remarks that he comes down on the side of those who see chance as a reflection of human ignorance. Nevertheless he saw things more clearly than many of those who came after. He distinguishes two modes of God's action. First, the direct and predictable course of events 'which Art and Industry have in a good part discovered, whose effects we may fortel. . . . ' On the other hand 'There is another way, full of Meanders and Labyrinths, . . . this we call Fortune, that serpentine and crooked line, whereby he draws those actions his wisdom intends, in a more unknown and secret way'.[10] However, near as this comes to the recognition of a real role for chance, it is clear where the author thinks the real truth lies ' . . . for even in sortilegies and matters of greatest uncertainty, there is a settled and preordered course of effects. It is we that are blind, not Fortune: because our Eye is too dim to discover the mystery of her effects, we foolishly paint her blind, and hoodwink the Providence of the Almighty'.[11]

According to Hooykaas, Sebastian Basso, writing in 1621, allowed 'that atoms move by chance and not according to a final aim'[12] at the same time as maintaining that God's purposeful activity was to be found on the religious or metaphysical level. This was a remarkable insight at such an early date in that it allowed the reality of chance without excluding God. It would be interesting to know if this is an isolated instance.

Whatever the case may be it is to A. R. Peacocke[13] in his 1978 Bampton lectures that we must turn for an explicit statement from a scientist of how God and chance might each be accorded their due. He sees God as having made a deliberate choice to use chance as a way of realizing the potentiality implicit in the creation. The giant lottery of the universe is used to sort through the whole gamut of possibilities and so discover those that are both viable and expressive of God's purpose. As we noted in Chapter 2, Peacocke counters Monod's arguments about the consequences of chance in the evolutionary process by drawing attention to the more recent work of Eigen and others which suggests that the emergence of life in some form may have been highly probable. What he also does is to suggest a reason for the adoption of this somewhat erratic way of steering the creation to its destined end. He claims that it is God's way of realizing the potential already implicit. Even though I believe this to be on the right lines, it is open to criticism. Pailin,[14] for example, although attracted by the idea which in some respects harmonizes with the process theology he favours, suggests that it smacks of deism. This is not the old deism in which the universe is likened to a machine wound up at the beginning and left to run unattended. It is nevertheless a randomization machine which still, apparently, does not depend on the direct involvement of God to achieve his ends. This is a serious criticism but it is one which is primarily concerned with God's providence to which we come in the next chapter. There is a further criticism and this is that it is not obvious whether there has been enough time for all the possibilities to be investigated and for the right ones to come to fruition. The lifetime of the universe is conditioned by the physical processes of which it is made up and the sorting process, necessary for life to emerge somewhere, would presumably have to be an order of magnitude shorter. In any case, on Peacocke's own account the shuffling of which we are speaking is not like that of balls in a bag. It is an immensely more complicated set of processes in which higher forms emerge from the lower. This makes it very difficult to see whether or not it is a plausible explanation.

Swinburne has also recognized the possibility that there might be genuine indeterminacy in nature. This would require that 'if God is creator of the Universe this can only be because he keeps nature indeterministic. It is not incompatible with his being creator of the universe that he should allow the existence of an element of chance in nature.'[15] However, we need to show rather more than that God and chance are not logically incompatible. We hope to show that there are positive reasons for supposing that an element of pure chance would play a constructive role in creating a richer environment than would otherwise be possible.

Advantages of the hypothesis that God uses chance

Here we shall attempt to take a God's-eye view of the creation and try to set out some advantages and disadvantages of incorporating a degree of indeterminism. The aim will be to show that chance offers the potential Creator many advantages which it is difficult to envisage being obtained in any other way. Because there are also penalties, the final reckoning must attempt to assess whether the gains outweigh the losses. In doing this we shall draw heavily on the technical results of the last chapter, making particular use of the analogical value of the examples in the section on the 'uses of chance'.

First we re-iterate the point that chance processes can lead to determinate ends. As many of the laws of nature are statistical, there is every reason to suppose that a Creator wishing to achieve certain ends might choose to reach them by introducing random processes whose macro-behaviour would have the desired character. If it could also be shown that the random strategy had other useful by-products so much the better.

Assuming that one prime aim of creation is to produce intelligent beings capable of interaction with their Creator, it is clearly necessary to have an environment which will develop their qualities in a God-like direction. It must stimulate their creative potentialities by generating interest and curiosity. It must give them scope for exercising their independence and free choice. It must be capable of presenting them with new and challenging situations to temper and strengthen their qualities. It can only do this if there is an element of the unexpected without which it would be impossible to experience surprise, excitement and challenge. The game which involves both skill and chance provides a simple model for what is required. Just as the experience of games in childhood, and tests and examinations of all kinds in later life develop our skills and personalities so we may expect that God, working on a larger canvas may have found it necessary to incorporate analogous features into the creation. Chance in our environment provides both the stimulus and the testing to promote our spiritual evolution.

Another requirement that one might expect is that the creation should display a true, if incomplete, picture of its Creator. People destined for fellowship with God ought not to find that they are misled by what they observe around them about his nature. This is not to suggest that mankind should expect to read the whole truth about God in the book of nature. Merely that it should not deliberately mislead. This implies that science must be possible. What is validly inferred from our experiments and experience must be a fragment of the whole truth. What is observed at one place at a given time must be re-producible at other times in other places. It must be possible to 'protect' our inferences by appropriate experimental design from interference from extraneous and uncontrolled factors which might vitiate our conclusions. God must deny himself the right to disturb the experimental conditions so that the scientists' faith in the trustworthiness of nature shall not be undermined. All of these features are ensured in a world where nature is neutral and is not used as the vehicle for arbitrary acts on the part of the Creator. The scientific game is not a game against an adversary but against nature.

If individuals are to be free, then allowance must be made for the fact that they will be able to interfere with natural processes and thwart (in some degree at least) the Creator's intention. The creation must therefore be made, as far as possible, 'idiot proof'. It must have a built-in capacity to recover from whatever man can do to it. Two possibilities appear to be open to a Creator. One is to foresee all possible decisions that all individuals everywhere might make, together with all their consequences and then to pre-programme the system to cope with the situations that arise. A second and more elegant alternative is to build in a capacity to respond to anything that may happen. A good case can be made out for believing that a sophisticated random process has just this capacity. Randomness implies variety and variety ensures that there is always the potential to grasp opportunities which the environment offers. For example, the human body is liable to be invaded by viruses of diseases such as influenza. Random mutations in the virus constantly make the body's defence mechanism obsolete. An immune system which was designed to cope with all conceivable mutations would be extraordinarily complicated. It would also be unnecessary. The same job can be done much more easily by a system which can allow the more successful of the varied range of anti-bodies present to multiply disproportionately in response to the invasion. Another example is provided by minor ecological disasters. The plants in an area will achieve an equilibrium with one another and their environment. If that equilibrium is disturbed by a change in the local environment (through fire or flood, say), those members of the surviving population most fitted to survive will rapidly multiply and fill the vacuum created. It is the great variety of types – even of a single species – which are the products of random mutations which ensure that some at least will be capable of carrying on. And so it is that the scars left on the countryside by industry are quickly healed when activity ceases, even to the extent of plants flourishing on what, to the mainstream of the population, would be toxic soil.

The survival of any group of living things depends on there being present in it a sufficient variety of forms to ensure that some at least are capable of prospering in any environment which is likely to appear. An effective way of ensuring the requisite degree of variety is for there to be a random element in the reproductive system which ensures the continual appearance of variant forms. It is not suggested that survival can be guaranteed by this means. The disaster may be so drastic as to prevent any adaptation by this or any other means. What can be claimed for randomness in the system is that it provides an inherent degree of robustness because of its ability to respond to unpredictable changes.

A similar phenomenon is apparent in social, as well as biological, systems. Societies adapt to change if their structures are sufficiently flexible to respond to social pressures and new ideas. By encouraging diversity of talent and interest they equip themselves to take advantage of new opportunities. By contrast, structurally rigid and ideologically monolithic societies are more prone to overthrow or internal convulsion because they do not have the internal variety generated by individual freedom which is necessary for survival.

It may be objected that we are arguing that the variety flowing from randomness is needed to cope with uncertainty in the environment. Would it have not been simpler to do without all uncertainty in the first place and so render the need for this provision unnecessary? That might be so in an inanimate world, but the starting point for our discussion was the unpredictability introduced by free human choice. Nevertheless, as the above examples show there might be considerable benefits from coping with unpredictability at all levels in the same fashion.

It might seem to be going too far to claim that a world of chance displays the moral character of God but here again the very neutrality of nature testifies to the 'fairness' or justice of God. Perhaps the most serious challenge to the Christian view of God as a loving father comes from undeserved suffering. Earthquake and famine and all manner of natural disasters are difficult to reconcile with one who cares for each individual and wills only their good. The force of this criticism is weakened somewhat if it is not necessary to see every single occurrence as the deliberate act of God. Such a view does, of course, raise other problems to which we shall come later but the statement of Jesus that his heavenly Father 'sends the rain on the honest and the dishonest' (Matt. 5.45), is one way of expressing the principle of fairness which results from the use of chance both in homely games and on the cosmic scale.

Our intention thus far has been to show that not only does the scientific account of the world require a real place for chance, but that there are good reasons for expecting a God of the kind envisaged by Christian theology to create just such a world. There are, of course, arguments on the other side. These centre on whether such a world is sufficiently under control to do justice to God's omnipotence. If there is an element of unpredictability it has to be allowed that things may not turn out as God intended – that the whole thing might go disastrously wrong or never even have got off the ground in the first place. Can we allow that God could fail? Such questions are intimately bound up with God's Providence. That is with the extent to which he is constantly involved in the processes of the world and the power which he has to super-impose his will on the waywardness of the system which he brought into being. We shall deal with this in the next chapter but here we indicate something of what is at stake.

We have argued that there is good reason for believing that in spite of the random path which evolution takes, the ends may be determinate. In particular, that the emergence of intelligent life capable of writing and reading books like this may have been virtually certain. It is not absolutely certain, however, though obviously it was possible. Could God have contemplated creating a vast universe which might have failed to produce life? I believe that it would weaken the case for a purposeful God if it could be shown, as Monod seems to have supposed, that life of a kind suitable for God's purposes was not certain to arise somewhere in the universe. But it would by no means destroy it. Given that life is a possible outcome it can be made as near certain as we wish by trying the experiment sufficiently often. It does diminish God somewhat if we admit that he could fail at anything he attempted – even though by repetition he would certainly succeed in the end. But this presupposes that he could have devised some means of getting it right first time. It may be that the whole conception of creation was (had to be?) of such stupendous proportions as to tax even the resources of an infinitely powerful God. The wastefulness of it all as it appears to economic man is, perhaps, of no significance if unlimited resources and power are available.

Even allowing that creation was certain to produce life in due course there were still risks to be faced. Suppose a giant meteorite had collided with the earth and wiped out God's handiwork in a moment? Or if, within the span of evolutionary history, biochemical events had taken a different course at some critical juncture. Suppose that the plot to murder Hitler in 1944 had been successful or that Jesus had contracted a fatal attack of smallpox in his teens or that a finger should accidentally press the nuclear button. If the view of creation that we have been advocating is anywhere near correct, all of these, and many other, possibilities are real and potentially crippling for the divine plan. The traditional Christian answer (supposing the premises to be allowed) is that such things, if they are crucial, would be taken care of by God's Providence. That he would have protected the infant Jesus or diverted the meteorite so that his plan could go forward. For many of the lesser disasters things could be put right in the fuller and richer world to which this one is the prelude. Alternatively, and in the spirit of the foregoing discussion, there would be the option of trying again but this raises the serious question of whether a moral God would discard whole imperfect universes in the casual manner of a child casting off an old toy in the hope of getting one which was just right.

A more serious alternative is that there are some risks that even God must take and that things really could have gone wrong leaving God's purpose thwarted. Indeed it would be possible to argue that they *did* go wrong in human history and that the story of redemption is the account of God's action to restore matters.

Although these objections are real ones, they do not, I contend, undermine the central thesis that a world of chance is not merely consistent with a theistic view of nature but, almost, required by it. To take this idea seriously is to write a considerable agenda for theologians but it does not deny the presuppositions on which their work rests.

At the end of the last chapter we raised the question of whether there was any such thing as pure chance, and we must now return to the answer we gave and set it in its theological context. Our conclusion there was that we could never ultimately know whether what we observe is a pseudo-random process generated by deterministic means or whether there was no causal mechanism whatever. From a theological point of view there is little at stake as long as it is allowed that God's is the ultimate responsibility for chance being there. Its *effect* is the same whatever the mode of its generation. That being said it is difficult to conceive of how God could be 'responsible' in some sense for pure chance without having designed the mechanism giving rise to it. Speaking personally, I find it impossible to frame any statement about God's action in generating random events which avoids the notion of design on his part and so justifies us in saying that chance events are without any explanation whatsoever. It is more congenial to both faith and reason to suppose that God generates the requisite degree of randomness much as we do, by deterministic means. We emphasize again that this does not imply or require fore-knowledge of the consequences at the micro-level on God's part. He is concerned with the macro-effects. The uncertainty at the micro-level provides the built-in flexibility needed to make the system adaptive and responsive.

(In passing I may add that this is not intended to provide a fundamental analysis of the nature of chance. At bottom, I think this is bound up with the notion of independence rather than lack of cause. Randomness then arises from the interaction of simultaneous but independent processes. To allow the existence of pure chance in any sense is rather like saying that God can choose to act so that his left hand does not know what his right is doing. Or to put it more formally: that there must be sources of independent action within the one Godhead. There seems to be nothing logically impossible in such a suggestion but whether or not it can be usefully developed is not clear.)

The Old Testament

The Bible is not a rich source of material from which to fashion a theology of chance. Indeed a cursory examination might suggest that what it does have to say is more akin to pre-scientific superstition and directly opposed to the view of nature that has begun to emerge in the earlier part of this chapter. If the text which MacKay quotes from Proverbs 16.33: 'The lots may be cast into the lap but the issue depends wholly on the Lord' is taken as definitive, there is little room for argument. To take the Bible seriously is to line up with those who claim that all chance is the product of ignorance. Certainly this is the way that it has traditionally been interpreted, anything less being seen as limiting God's power. However, we question whether even the Old Testament will unequivocally support such a view. It certainly contains many references to the casting of lots, but the interpretation to be put on these events is not always unambiguous as we shall see. Equally the Bible stories are full of incidents of an apparently accidental character into which are read signs of divine action. But against this must be set other occasions where a real role for chance, as opposed to God, seems to be envisaged. We shall therefore take a closer look to see whether any biblical support can be found for the God of chance to which our reasoning has been leading.

It has to be allowed that the evidence is slender and that many of the incidents concerned are susceptible to interpretations other than those we shall put upon them. It is difficult to know how far we can fathom the minds of those in biblical times who lived in a culture so different from our own. This consideration applies, of course, to both sides of the argument. All that we seek to show is that there is not a single biblical view and, especially when we come to the New Testament, that it is far from being totally opposed to a theistic view that could be supported by scientific presuppositions.

Let us begin with the casting of lots where what we should call chance is quite explicit. Casting lots to reach decisions was commonplace in the ancient world and the Jews were no exception. Rabinovitch[16] has examined the practice in Jewish literature within and beyond the bounds of the Old Testament; David[17] also has much material of interest.

Lots were sometimes cast as part of religious ritual as, for example, to decide which of two goats should be selected as the sin-offering and which should be sent out into the wilderness (Lev. 16.9). Sometimes the object was to share out land as when Joshua divided up the land among the people of Israel 'Joshua cast lots for them in Shiloh before the Lord and distributed the land there to the Israelites in their proper shares' (Josh. 18.10). The advantages of such a procedure were recognized in the proverb 'Cast lots, and settle a quarrel, and so keep litigants apart' (Prov. 18.18). In a somewhat different vein, lots were used to find the guilty person. One example concerns Saul's campaign against the Philistines. Saul wanted to make a night attack but the priest advised caution suggesting that God be consulted first. However, no reply was forthcoming so Saul concluded that God must be withholding his reply on account of sin among his people. Saul and Jonathan stood on one side and the rest of the Israelites on the other. Then Saul said to God 'Why hast thou not answered thy servant today? If this guilt lie in me or in my son Jonathan, O Lord God of Israel, let the lot be Urim; if it lie in thy people Israel, let it be Thummim' (I Sam. 14.41). The lot fell on the side of Saul and Jonathan and then a second trial had to be made to decide between the two of them. This time the lot fell on Jonathan who thereupon admitted to a minor misdemeanour. Exactly what Urim and Thummim were is not clear. They might have been two objects, like black and white balls, or two sides of a single object, like the head and tail of a coin. What is clear is that they were some randomizing device through which God's will might be revealed. A similar approach to finding the guilty party was made on board the ship taking Jonah to Tarshish. When a storm threatened to break up the ship ' . . . the sailors said to each other, "Come and let us cast lots to find out who is to blame for this bad luck." So they cast lots, and the lot fell on Jonah' (Jonah 1.7).

The most obvious interpretation of these events is that the Israelites, and many of their contemporaries, saw all events as determined by God and, hence, that he could be prevailed upon to reveal his will in the outcome of a lottery. Such an interpretation is reinforced by Jonathan's admission of guilt. However, there is another strand of thinking that can be detected in these examples which suggests that other considerations may have played a part. For example in dividing up the land the use of lots eliminated all human bias. That such procedures were fair would be based on the cumulative experience that no systematic biasses occurred. Rabinovitch produces arguments to show that such primitive ideas of probability theory were understood by those who used lotteries.[18] If this is so then it must have been realized that there was a certain neutrality in God's dealings. If Urim and Thummim did occur in a random sequence, there would have been some long term pattern in the decisions arrived at.

There is another possible interpretation of the Jonah story which Rabinovitch attributes to Rabbi ben Masheh Aramah (fifteenth century). According to him the use of the plural for lots implies that lots were cast several times and that each time the lot fell on Jonah.[19] If this were true then the interpretation would be rather different. For the lot to fall on Jonah *every* time would be a significant departure from randomness. The finger of God would then be seen not in the chance happening but in the otherwise inexplicable deviation from what would be expected if chance alone were operating. God is then seen not so much as determining the fall of the lots in the ordinary course of events but, on special occasions, indicating his choice by interfering with the otherwise random process.

The view that chance might exist alongside God's action seems to have existed in Philistine religion. In the story recounted in I Sam. 6 the Philistines had captured the Ark. Subsequently there had been unpleasant visitations of rats and tumours. It was only natural for them to suppose that these had come upon them at the instigation of Israel's God. They therefore set up an experiment to see whether he was to blame. Two cows which had never been yoked were attached to a cart containing gifts and the cart was then released. 'Watch it: if it goes up towards its own territory to Beth-shemesh, then it is the Lord who has done us this great injury; but if not, then we shall know that his hand has not touched us, but we have been victims of chance' (I Sam. 6.9). God and chance could evidently co-exist.[20]

There is another class of event which is very close to decision by lot. Appeal was sometimes made to omens, rather than dice. Accidental happenings were invested with great significance in the belief that God was using them as signs. This too is consistent with the view that even such trivial events were expressing the direct and deliberate choices of God. However, once again, it is not clear whether all such events were to be so regarded or only those few when a special appeal for guidance had been made. In any case the terms of the trial were set up and interpreted on man's side. Earlier in the story of Urim and Thummim quoted above Jonathan and his armour-bearer had hoped that God would deliver the Philistines into their hands. Whether God was to do so was to be decided by the two of them going to within range of the Philistines and hearing what they had to say. 'If they say, "Stay where you are till we come to you", then we will stay where we are and not go up to them. But if they say, "Come up to us", we will go up; this will be the sign that the Lord has put them into our power' (I

Sam. 14.9–10). Another interesting example is provided by the case of Gideon's fleece. Gideon wanted a sign from God. He put a fleece of wool on the threshing floor and told God that if the dew was to be found on the fleece and not on the floor he would read that as a sign of God's approval. And so it happened. Not satisfied with one trial, Gideon wanted confirmation so he set up a second test. This time dew on the ground and not on the fleece was to be the positive response. 'God let it be so that night: the fleece alone was dry, and on all the ground there was dew' (Judg. 6.33–40). Gideon clearly wanted something which did not allow the suspicion that what happened the first night was merely accidental. By asking for the reverse sign on the second night he demanded something which, in the ordinary course, would be highly improbable. It seems that one odd occurrence could be just chance; it took two to put it beyond reasonable doubt (shades of the significance test logic!).

These are admittedly fragmentary, even if suggestive, pieces of evidence on which to challenge the view that in the Old Testament there is no such thing as chance. A much clearer alternative view is found in the Wisdom literature. Doubts about everything being under God's benificent control were expressed by the 'Speaker' in Ecclesiastes. ' . . . I understood that the righteous and the wise and all their doings are under God's control; but is it love or hatred? No man knows. Everything that confronts him, everything is empty, since one and the same fate befalls everyone, just and unjust alike, good and bad, clean and unclean, the man who offers sacrifice and the man who does not. . . . This is what is wrong in all that is done here under the sun: that one and the same fate befalls every man. . . . One more thing I have observed here under the sun: speed does not win the race nor strength the battle. Bread does not belong to the wise, nor wealth to the intelligent, nor success to the skilful; time and chance govern all' (Eccles. 9. 1–3, 11). In short, nature is not geared to meting out justice to individuals, it is neutral. This passage might easily be dismissed as typical of the author's cynicism but for the fact that it anticipates some words of Jesus as well as showing an accurate assessment of the human condition. A comprehensive view of the Old Testament must reckon with the observations of the speaker as well as the pronouncements of the prophets.

There are also other Old Testament passages which have been held to say something about the place of chance in nature. For example, Macquarrie sees Ps. 104.24–25 as showing a view of nature which finds room for purposeless activity. 'Thou hast made all by thy wisdom; and the earth is full of thy creatures, beasts great and small. Here is a great immeasurable sea, in which move creatures beyond number. Here ships sail to and fro, here is Leviathan whom thou hast made thy plaything.'[21] Macquarrie's interpretation rests on an alternative reading for 'thy plaything' which says 'that it may sport in it'. This attribution of freedom to the animal kingdom is certainly consistent with a less rigid understanding of how God manages nature but such poetic forms of expression can provide only the slenderest of threads on which to hang a theology of nature.

The New Testament

In the New Testament a rather different emphasis occurs whether we look at individual instances or the broad attitude to natural happenings. However, the arguments are not all on one side. On the one hand God's concern with the details of creation is clear enough. Jesus said 'Are not sparrows two a penny? Yet without your Father's leave not one of them can fall to the ground. As for you, even the hairs of your head have all been counted' (Matt. 10.29–31, see also Luke 12.6–7). But, echoing Ecclesiastes he also speaks of ' . . . your heavenly Father, who makes his sun rise on good and bad alike, and sends the rain on the honest and the dishonest' (Matt. 5.45). The neutrality of the weather treating all alike is an expression of that neutrality and fairness which is characteristic of random phenomena. This same equality of approach to all his children was sometimes puzzling to those steeped in the Old Testament. They assumed that individual misfortunes must be attributed directly to God. So when a tower fell in Siloam killing eighteen innocent people an explanation seemed called for. Jesus made it clear that they were no more guilty than others (Luke 13.4). The same was true of those massacred by Pilate (Luke 13.1, 2), of the crippled woman (Luke 13.16) and the man born blind (John 9.3). In each case Jesus denied that the event or the condition was a deliberate act of punishment aimed at particular people. When he does give a reason, the affliction is attributed to Satan or is represented as providing an opportunity for God's healing purpose to be displayed. In the cases of the tower and the massacre, Jesus uses the incidents to point out that everyone is liable to such happenings and that they should have the effect of moving people to repentance.

The two sides of the case are not necessarily inconsistent. The message seems to be that although God is *concerned* about everything that happens (for example the death of a sparrow), not all happenings are his deliberate acts though all provide opportunities for his real nature to be revealed. There are other forces at work – whether we personify them as Satan or attribute them to natural processes – which thwart his purposes. In a world in which there is a real element of randomness, as we have seen, there are things which are bound to happen even though the particular circumstances of their occurring cannot be predicted. This is not so far removed in its outlook from Jesus' saying 'Alas for the world that such causes of stumbling arise! Come they must, but woe betide the man through whom they come.' (Matt. 18.7), or, of Judas 'The Son of Man is going the way appointed for him in the scriptures; but alas for that man by whom the Son of Man is betrayed! It would be better for that man if he had never been born' (Mark 14.21). Although these things cannot be avoided, that does not absolve those responsible from blame; the blame should certainly not be laid at God's door. Those who take a more deterministic view of things might have wanted to say in the story of the Good Samaritan 'The Lord designed that a priest should be going down by the same road'. Jesus said, 'It so happened that a priest . . . ' (or 'by chance' AV).

Whatever interpretation is put upon these various incidents – and they are often peripheral to the main point – they certainly do not require the belief that every event, however trivial, must express a particular intention of God and thus reflect, sometimes adversely, on his character. On the contrary there is enough indeterminism both for individual autonomy and for accidents to happen. Chance is not ruled out.

We have left on one side the most obvious New Testament support for the 'old' view, namely the use of lots in Acts 1.26. This concerns the choice of a successor to replace Judas in the ranks of the apostles. It was not, of course, a random selection from an unlimited field. To be eligible, a candidate had to have been a member of the group who had accompanied Jesus from the beginning. The field had been narrowed down to Joseph and Matthias before lots were used. Even then prayer was offered first asking God to declare by this means which he had chosen. Casting lots was a natural way to resolve a difficult issue and one for which there were ample precedents. For our purposes the incident seems to show that the apostles believed that God could affect the fall of the lot. (It could also be held to show, not that God determined the fall of the lot, but, foreseeing what the outcome would be, he influenced the minds of the apostles to attach the name of the chosen candidate to the lot which would emerge.) This is not the same as saying that God ordinarily concerned himself with such things, why else should prayer have been necessary? The most that can be claimed is that God is capable of such action. It is not legitimate to infer that he is directly involved in all such events.

There is, however, a deeper reason for seeing a world in which chance is real as more consistent with the Gospel story. The world into which Jesus was born was subject, as it still is, to suffering, disaster and misfortune of all kinds. It is clear that Jesus saw these things as opposed to his Father's will and he spent his ministry in showing by word and action a better way. There was a price to be paid for putting things right. God in Jesus Christ took the consequences upon himself, as the crucifixion bears witness. One can view this, as some theologies do, as a divine transaction planned to the last detail to satisfy some basic principle of justice. It is not a view which easily commends itself to the scientific mind. It is true that much of the suffering can be attributed to man's exercising his own freedom, but not all events, especially natural disasters, can be seen in this way. There seems to be a residuum of mischances which are part of the very nature of things. To attribute them to Satan does not really explain anything. It is not particularly difficult to believe in a personal devil or even in demonic forces, but even if such exist it is not easy to attribute to them the power to cause volcanic eruptions or droughts. There are problems enough, as we shall see, in attributing such powers of intervention to God himself. It seems more reasonable to suppose that a world with all the properties necessary for it to fulfil God's purposes could not avoid being one in which accidents happen. One of the purposes of the incarnation would then have been to demonstrate the difference between God's true nature and the accidental and harmful accompaniments of creation. This Jesus did in healing the sick, feeding the hungry and, supremely, by suffering crucifixion and rising again.

The church

Until recently there appears to have been little serious effort among theologians to grapple with the problems for faith of living in a world in which uncertainty and accident form an integral part. Doubtless this is because there was seen to be no problem. Everything was in the hand of God and to suggest otherwise would have been to question his omnipotence. Indeed, where the matter has been discussed, a rather rigid Old Testament view has usually been taken with no recognition of the more flexible understanding we detected in parts of the Old Testament and in the New. The notable and significant exception to this rule is St Thomas Aquinas. He discusses chance in his *Summa Contra Gentiles*.[22] There is a passing reference in Book 2, Chapter xxxix which is concerned with establishing that the distribution of things is not from chance. The discussion allows that chance exists and even that 'there may be chance in the making of things produced from matter' and 'perhaps chance causes the distinction of certain individuals'. But the more important and positive statement is in Book 3, Chapter LXXIV 'That Divine Providence Does Not Exclude Chance or Luck'. He claims to have proved in Chapter LXXII that it would be inconsistent with Divine Providence if all things happened of necessity. Consequently, it would also be inconsistent with divine providence if there were no luck or chance in the world. Of the various arguments adduced in support of the proposition of the chapter title is one that the intention of an individual cause cannot possibly extend to all possible contingencies and it is through things happening beside the intention of the agent that things occur by chance. And Ecclesiastes 9.11 is quoted in support. Most other writers have gone along with Sir Thomas More in asserting that there is no such thing as chance. In its *Directory for the Publique Worship of God*,[23] published in 1645, the Westminster Assembly was quite specific ' . . . that diseases come not by chance . . . , but by the wise and orderly guidance of the good hand of God to every particular person smitten by them'. Nearly two centuries later in 1821 there appeared, anonymously, *The New Whole Duty of Man*, as a corrective to the *Whole Duty of Man* of Cromwell's time. The author puts the matter so comprehensively and uncompromisingly that it is worth quoting at length. He writes:

> So that what the vanity of science, falsely so called, has ascribed to nature, or to second causes, exclusively of the first; and what men vulgarly call chance, or unforeseen accident; is in scripture resolved into the immediate will and providence of God. Thus, when a person is slain by chance or accident, as men vulgarly speak, the scripture more accurately expresses it, saying that God *delivered* such a one *into the hand* of him that slew him without design: Exod. 21.13. and in *all other* instances the same notion is everywhere kept up in scripture. Neither is it merely in a pious manner of expression that the scripture ascribes every event to the providence of God; but it is strictly and philosophically true in nature and reason, that there is no such thing as chance or accident: it being evident that those words do not signify any thing really existing, any thing that is truly an agent, or the cause of any event; but they signify merely men's ignorance of the real and immediate cause

– and so on, in similar vein including –

> . . . the supreme power of God directing by his omnipresent providence, the inanimate motions of the whole material and unintelligent world.[24]

We may question whether in '*all other* instances the same notion is everywhere kept up in scripture' but this passage undoubtedly sums up what has commonly been believed. Pope expressed this philosophy in verse which has been quoted with approval from many a pulpit:

> All nature is but art, unknown to thee;
> All chance, direction which thou canst not see;
> All discord, harmony not understood;
> All partial evil, universal good.[25]

This view has not been significantly modified by scientific thinking. Both MacKay, as already noted, and Pollard, as we shall see in the next chapter, adopt positions which, for all practical purposes deny that chance is real. In fact, there is a striking parallel between the views of the *New Whole Duty of Man* and a contemporary writer on science and religion. Yarnold writes:

> If the Purpose of God is the ultimate cause of the phenomena of the physical world, then events on the most fundamental level are not irrational. Every electron is held in existence by God. Every electron moves in exact obedience to God's Will. If, as we believe, physical science really has reached the fundamental level beyond which it is impossible to trace back the causal sequence any further, then may not this be the very point at which God's control over the universe is exercised? Is not the statistical regularity of large-scale phenomena the logical result of the direct control which God exercises over countless individual particles on the microscopic scale? Are not the extremely rare departures from the statistical regularity of large-scale phenomena (departures which are not ruled out from the strictly scientific point of view) the occasions of the direct personal action of God in a universe in which he usually acts impersonally?[26]

Yarnold leaves no scope at all for pure chance, but the distinction he draws between personal and impersonal action is capable of being accommodated within the frame-work here proposed. We return to the matter in the next chapter.

St Thomas Aquinas apart, these examples gleaned from many quarters, speak with one voice: God is in charge of everything and chance does not exist. But actions are often a surer guide to what people really believe than what theologians write. We therefore turn to see how Christians have reacted in the face of uncertainty.

It is hardly surprising that those sections of the church which have modelled their practice most closely on the Bible should resort to decision by lots. However, their use was not taken lightly and was sometimes the subject of dispute. The idea of a deterministic world can go happily in hand with a Calvinistic theology, but even that doughty Arminian John Wesley resorted to lots – no doubt following the biblical precedents. One of the best known examples concerned the choice of a wife when he was in Georgia. The circumstances are recorded in his Journal for 4 March 1737 and the matter is also discussed by David in *Games, Gods and Gambling*.[27] Being unable to make up his mind, John and his friend Mr Delamotte cast lots to settle the matter – with a result unfavourable to the match. They had first prayed that a 'perfect lot' might be given and David infers that a 'bad lot' would mean that not enough prayer had been offered and hence provide a way out if the outcome was unpalatable. This seems to be a mis-reading of the situation. John goes on to say, in effect, that he resorted to lots because his 'heart was not wholly resigned to His will. Therefore not daring to depend on my own judgment, I cried the more earnestly to Him to supply what was wanting in me'. It sounds as if the matter was so delicately balanced in his mind that the resort to sortilege provided a welcome relief. David also remarks that 'Wesley's sect' was unusual in retaining sortilege. By contrast, the Catholic Apostolic Church had condemned sortilege as of pagan origin. However, this curious fragment of Christianity was not founded until the 1830s, and can hardly be regarded as the authoritative voice of the church catholic. But David is certainly correct in saying that sortilege was practised in early Methodism and it continued after Wesley's death. John used lots to decide whether to preach in Bristol at Whitefield's invitation – after having opened the Bible at random and received no guidance.[28] In 1735 brother Charles entered into an agreement with his friends that when they were equally divided on any matter the issue would be decided by lot, though whether the outcome was to be regarded as the decision of God is not clear.[29]

Shortly after John's death the Conference resorted to lots on the vexed question of whether the administration of the sacraments was to be restricted to those preachers who were Methodist clergymen of the Church of England. The conference letter makes it clear that the Conference was deeply divided on the matter and wished to preserve its unity in the face of a difficult decision. The biblical authority claimed was the familiar Prov. 16.33 but also Prov. 18.18, 'The lot causeth contentions to cease, and parteth between the mighty' (AV). It apparently succeeded in keeping the peace and the use of lots says a good deal for their common sense if not their theology.[30]

The episode was also referred to by the Bishop of London in his 'Twelve lectures on the Acts of the Apostles in relation to the choice of Judas's successor' which suggests that the established church took a more cautious view. Reporting the matter in 1828 the *Methodist Magazine*[31] made it clear that Methodists were not pleased with the Bishop's criticism of their use of lots in the matter of the sacrament. But although he regarded the Methodist action to be rash and presumptuous, the bishop allowed that the case of choosing a new apostle involved a method of reaching a decision which was appointed by God himself in the Law.

The practice of deciding religious matters by lot has not completely died out even in official circles. The selection of the pope of the Coptic Orthodox Church is made by a boy drawing one of three slips of paper from a chalice. The rules and discipline of the Ontario Amish Mennonite Conference provides that 'if more than the required number of candidates (for the ministry) are voted for by the church the lots shall be used to decide whom the Lord has chosen'.[32] The Hutterians in Alberta and Manitoba also used lots for ministerial choice. Here also, one suspects faithfulness to biblical practice rather than a worked out theology lies behind the practice.

Opening the Bible 'at random' in the search for divine guidance has been widely practised from St Francis onwards, sometimes with amusing results, but it is doubtful whether any but the more extreme sects take it seriously nowadays.

It is not unusual to find contradictory beliefs about chance in popular religious thinking. In some sections of the Christian church gambling has been condemned, and even games of chance regarded with suspicion. This has not only been on the ground of the social and personal cost which over-indulgence causes, nor on the socialist principle that the unequal distribution of wealth without regard to need is a bad thing. There has also been the feeling that there is something intrinsically evil about chance. Yet within the same religious circles random opening of the Bible and a highly developed sense of Providence has seen God's hand in all other events however trivial. Within living memory there were those who regarded insurance as wrong because it attempted to thwart the will of God. (The Amish people also objected to insurance but on the grounds that it made merchandise of human lives for which they had other biblical evidence.)

These fascinating by-ways illustrate, more than anything else, that the generality of Christians have held various and sometimes inconsistent views about chance. This is true whether one looks at the formal theological treatises or at the practices of individual Christian bodies. The 'mind of the church' does not speak with a clear voice but Mary Baker Eddy spoke for many when she wrote:

Accidents are unknown to God, or immortal Mind, and we must
leave the mortal basis of belief and unite with the one Mind, in
order to change the notion of chance to the proper sense of God's
unerring direction and thus bring out harmony. Under divine
Providence there can be no accidents, since there is no room for
imperfection in perfection.[33]

Although the phraseology carries the overtones of Christian Science
the sentiments would command much support. It is interesting that a
recent commentator on these words, while purporting to agree with
them, in fact moves nearer to the main thesis of this chapter. He
wrote:

The view that life is determined by chance is also a mental model,
and its validity has been challenged by a more scientific view. That
challenge came from Christ Jesus. Instead of moving powerlessly
from circumstance to circumstance, he confronted chance, accident, disorder, with the law of God, the law of infinite ever-present
good.

He quotes the quelling of the storm, the healing of the blind and the
feeding of the multitude as examples of the purposefulness and
harmony of divine intelligence. 'Christ Jesus' works showed that God,
Spirit, is not the author of chaos and chance.'[34] Here chance appears
as an impersonal 'enemy' that has to be attacked. There is no hint as to
how chance is to be accounted for or how its presence is to be
reconciled with an all-good and powerful God. Nevertheless, it stakes
out a position in clear distinction to that of the founder of his sect and
to many main line Christians by allowing that chance is real and must
be found a place in any comprehensive theology.

A non-religious approach

The personification of chance was a natural enough way of accounting
for uncertainty. It provided an explanation by positing a cause for
apparently uncaused events. Even if we do not ascribe these things to
the goddesses Tyche or Fortuna, we still find it very difficult to speak
of chance without lapsing into the metaphysical error of speaking of
'Chance' as a causal agent. The various strands of biblical and
theological thought we have outlined above, whatever their failings,
do, on the whole, avoid this error. It is therefore mildly surprising to
find an attempt of a pseudo-scientific character to invest chance with a
purposeful character which is not so far removed from personification. This seems to be the intention of Arthur Koestler who has
championed the view that there is more to chance than meets the eye.

He does not pretend, of course, to offer a theology of chance but if there were anything in Koestler's ideas they would certainly be relevant for the fashioning of a theology. For example, if his view were true that there exists (or may exist) an a-causal world (whatever that means) in parallel with the causal world we know, there would be important implications for the character and nature of God.

Koestler's idea seems to be that the quirks and twists which turn up in ESP experiments and in the everyday experiences of coincidences may be indicative that traditional science provides a blinkered view of reality. Or, to put it another way, that the apparently a-causal happenings which we ascribe to chance are symptomatic of other dimensions of reality. Any theology which reckons only with the world as interpreted according to the scientific paradigm is thus seriously incomplete.

To illustrate this approach we consider the book by Hardy, Harvie and Koestler entitled *The Challenge of Chance*.[35] A somewhat fuller treatment of Koestler's thoughts are given in his book *The Roots of Coincidence*.[36]

The Challenge of Chance begins with an account of an attempt by Hardy and Harvie to investigate ESP by a series of experiments conducted at the Caxton Hall Westminster in 1967. Their aim was to transfer images or pictures from the minds of an audience to a group of subjects. The audience viewed the pictures projected on to a screen which could not be seen by the subjects. The question to be decided was whether or not the number of correct guesses made by the subjects was in excess of what would be expected by chance. This was not a straightforward matter since it is not easy to decide whether the correspondence between the subject's drawing and the picture (if any) is close enough to qualify as correct. However, this problem was satisfactorily solved by an experimental determination carried out to ensure that telepathy could not possibly be involved.

It is not relevant for our purposes to describe the experiments or the results in detail. Suffice it to say that the whole operation was conducted with meticulous care. The results were not sufficiently different from the chance prediction to infer that ESP was at work. Most experimenters would have regarded that as the end of the matter, but Hardy and Harvie noticed what they called evidence of coincident thoughts. It appeared that several subjects would some-times produce similar drawings or statements even though they bore no relation to the object being shown. This raised the question of whether images were being transmitted between subjects. Here again it is not easy to judge whether the number of coincidences was in excess of the expectation on the chance hypothesis because there is no well-defined population of objects from which the subjects can be supposed to be selecting their images. The calculations the authors were able to make suggested that there was no statistically significant evidence for telepathic communication between subjects. As a further check, 'imaginary' experiments were conducted using random numbers in order to see what would happen when the possibility of ESP was entirely eliminated. Here, to the authors' surprise they found that the number of coincidences was significantly larger than the chance prediction. Yet the result was purely the result of the random number sequence. Since telepathy was ruled out some other explanation had to be found. Inaccuracy in recording the number of coincidences – non-randomness in the digits or some form of para-normal influence – were ruled out as scarcely plausible. The authors concluded that 'chance' must be the explanation, and since the outcome was not that predicted by probability theory there must be something odd about chance. (They did not, apparently, query whether there might be something wrong with probability theory!).

At this point Koestler takes over with a catalogue of strange and 'meaningful' coincidences which are presumably intended to support the view that there is something odd about chance which cannot be explained within the framework of traditional science. Some of the coincidences related by Koestler are certainly very remarkable. But to show that something beyond our experience is at work requires one to establish, as Hardy and Harvie tried to do in their experiments, that such events occur more frequently than would be the case in the absence of the para-normal dimension. Koestler recognizes that this objection will be made but by-passes it by distinguishing between meaningful and unmeaningful coincidences; it is the former which demand some special explanation. He is apparently unmoved by the fact that probabilists such as Warren Weaver have experienced remarkable coincidences while claiming that no supernatural explanation is called for.[37] Koestler slyly wonders why such people re-tell their stories if they really believe that they signify nothing.

The experimental results of Hardy and Harvie and the anecdotal incidents described by Koestler are only very loosely related. The former boil down to the claim that the random numbers given in Lindley and Miller's Cambridge Elementary Statistical Tables and Fisher and Yates'[38] tables do not have the properties they 'ought' to have; the latter that some coincidences have a character that justifies the description 'meaningful'. Does this justify us in entertaining the idea that there might be an a-causal world in parallel to this one? Hardly. The most obvious explanation of Hardy and Harvie's results is that the set of random numbers they used show some deviation from randomness. Such deviations would be expected from time to time anyhow, but it is also possible that the methods of generating the numbers was slightly flawed in a manner shown up by this experiment. Hardy and Harvie reject this explanation on the grounds that this set of numbers had been subjected to rigorous tests of randomness. But different tests of randomness are designed to detect different kinds of departure from the random hypothesis, and it is always possible that a new test (such as those experiments provided) will bring to light some hitherto undetected non-random feature. Until their results are replicated using random numbers from other sources, this remains the most plausible explanation. We are certainly not justified in concluding that 'chance' does not conform to the laws of probability. In any case, since the laws of probability are supposed to describe chance phenomena this puts the boot on the wrong foot. We ought rather to be examining the axioms of probability and amending them so that they do the job for which they are designed as already noted. Koestler's meaningful coincidences likewise cannot begin to show that there is something odd about chance until evidence is forthcoming that they (meaningful or otherwise) are more numerous than can be expected on the current scientific world view.

It is certainly no part of a scientist's or a theologian's brief to deny the reality of the unseen or to discourage rigorous research into the paranormal. Nevertheless, it does the cause of religion no service when scientists stray over boundaries of their territory and discover mysteries where in all probability none exists. When a question is put to the test of experiment and the answer turns out to be a clear 'no' it is time to call a halt.

We have dealt with this particular subject at greater length than its intrinsic importance warrants, to illustrate the hazards that await those whose pre-disposition to accept a supernatural view of the world leads them to give undue credence to the results of pseudo-science, however well intentioned. There, doubtless, are more things in heaven and earth than are dreamed of in our philosophy. But, revelation apart, the rigorous and disciplined application of scientific method is the only sure way we have for discovering them.

Summary

We have ranged widely in our attempt to find a theistic understanding of creation which does justice to the scientific world view without undermining Christian belief. The central thesis of this chapter is summed up in its title – God of Chance. Chance is thus seen as a deliberate and, perhaps, necessary part of God's creation. At the outset we stated two criteria by which our attempt must be judged. We satisfied the first by taking the scientific account as our starting point, lining up with those scientists who regard chance as real and fundamental. This led us to the conclusion that since chance is such an integral part of creation, it must be part of God's plan. Thus we can agree that everything which happens is ultimately God's responsibility while denying that every single happening has a meaning in terms of God's intention. His purpose is rather to be seen in the aggregate effects of many such happenings. Our second criterion was concerned with how far this view of things could be harmonized with biblical theism and what implication it had for the character of God. We concluded that the record of scripture and the mind of the church gave no clear picture but, contrary to what many have supposed, there is much that is consonant with the line we have been taking. This is especially, and significantly, the case when we consider the life, teaching, death and resurrection of Jesus. To some the abandonment of the traditional idea, expressed by Pope or Browne, of an all-powerful God in intimate control of every electron and weaving an intricate pattern may seem a loss. But against this must be set the more subtle nature of the stochastic universe which is much richer in potential than the rigid mechanical model which we seek to replace. There is nothing that I can see in this view which limits God's ability to achieve his ultimate purposes. Whether or not his power to attain immediate objectives in evolution and history is restricted in a way which diminishes his greatness is, for the moment, an open question. If this were to be the case, the theological implications would be serious. Would it then be still meaningful to speak of his Providence?

6

Chance and Providence

The argument in the last chapter centred on the doctrine of creation. The aim was to see how the scientific picture of the world, in which chance plays a crucial role, could be reconciled with the Christian view that God created all things according to a plan. We aimed to show that it was possible to assert that there was a purpose even though the path which evolution has taken appears to be haphazard and undirected. The doctrine of creation was saved by arguing that a high degree of randomness in the evolutionary process was consistent with a determinate end and that there were positive advantages in creating an environment which is characterized by variety and unpredictability. However, in saving one doctrine, we were undermining another. For if we allow that things happen in the world that are not direct or intended acts of God – as the random hypothesis requires – then we are limiting the degree of control which he exercises. What then becomes of his Providence? Indeed, we have gone further by claiming that the lawful behaviour of so much of the natural world is no more than the result of chaotic undirected motion at the micro level. But it is on the lawfulness of nature that an important part of the doctrine of creation has been built. If this turns out to be a mere illusion of large numbers how can we speak of those laws as expressing God's intention?

The problem to be faced in this chapter is that of seeing whether it is possible to retain or re-state the Christian doctrine of providence within a theology which recognizes a significant element of pure chance in nature, and perhaps, in history. In Chapter 3 we dwelt at length on the meaning of chance. We must be equally clear what we mean by providence.

Providence

The idea of God's continual care for his creation and his involvement in its affairs is a central theme of the Old Testament and has been a prominent strand in Christian thought ever since. The literature of the subject is enormous and extends far beyond the particular concerns of the present chapter. A recent treatment of the topic which is sympathetic to the scientific world view and on which I shall freely draw is contained in Langford's book *Providence*. Langford classifies providence under several traditional heads of which three will serve to clarify the nature of the task that we face. These are general providence, special providence and miracle.[1]

General providence is concerned with God's overall responsibility for what happens in the world. It includes, for example, his bringing the world into being in a manner which gave rise to life and thought and his continuing to keep it in existence. In this last connection it is usually held that without God's sustaining power nothing could continue to exist and hence that a belief in his general providence is essential. In passing, this should, perhaps, be questioned. To me it is not self-evident, even if a supreme being was necessary to get things started, that there should be a continuing need for him to keep it going. Indeed common sense notions would suggest the opposite – that things continue in existence unless acted upon by some disturbing force. However that may be, there is nothing in the theology of chance set out in the last chapter which places a serious question mark against general providence in this sense. We postulated a purposeful God who designed the cosmos. The extent of, or need for, his day-to-day involvement in keeping that creation in being can remain an open question.

God's special providence, on the other hand, is concerned with more particular and local happenings. At each juncture of nature and history there are, typically, a number of choices open. All fall within the realm of the possible. If at such a juncture God deliberately steers events so as to achieve a particular end then that is an example of his special providence. There is no question of the miraculous since he has chosen one among several choices allowed by the laws of nature. What marks the action out is that through it God achieves some specific purpose which could not have been guaranteed without his intervention.

There is, of course, a fundamental problem about this definition because there is no certain way of establishing that such an event has actually happened. The gardener blessed with a shower after praying for rain may attribute his good fortune to the efficacy of his prayer, but the sceptic will not be impressed. He will point to the logical impossibility of proving that, without the prayer, the drought would have continued. He may add that, in all probability, the local tennis players were praying at the same time for a continuation of the sunshine. Nevertheless, religious literature abounds in the testimony of those who are convinced that such happenings have occurred and in some cases, at least, it must be allowed that a natural explanation seems no less incredible. Such alleged events certainly nourish faith and the circumstantial evidence may be strong. Here, however, we are concerned with the prior question of whether such acts are ruled out by the world view with which theology now has to reckon.

Without special providence Christian belief begins to crumble at the very point where it seems most relevant to individuals. For if God is powerless to affect the course of events, there is little point in intercessory prayer. What is the point of praying 'give us this day our daily bread' if nothing that God is able to do will affect the prospects of harvest? There is certainly a sense of security in the belief that God is keeping an eye on things and that he will step in if anything threatens to thwart his purposes. Even in the face of evil and undeserved suffering one can gain strength from the view that God has power to make things come right in the end. However the argument is about what is true and not what is comforting. If God is banished as an active partner in running his own world, and rendered impotent at the personal level, much that is distinctively Christian vanishes. Pope's picture[2] of the god at work behind the scenes is no more than a vain attempt to keep one's spirits up.

But is this really true? Is anything really vital lost if we admit that the guiding hand of God is a fiction; that in reality we are on our own until life's journey is over. The perceptive critic might go further and argue that the idea of special providence is a sign of imperfection in the creator. For if the cosmos had been properly designed in the first place, surely it would not be necessary for the creator to interfere. And even if he were able to do so, why should he want to? This argument would have some force in a deterministic world but that is not the kind of world we live in.

The essential reason why God should wish to intervene is that creation was not a once-and-for-all event in the distant past. Creation is a continuing process and God is therefore still at work bringing new things out of mind and matter. The evolutionary picture which emerges from the modern scientific world view is one of constant change and development. New forms of increasing complexity and potential have evolved. To speak of God 'interfering' or 'intervening' is to pre-judge the issue. The use of these words implies that creation was an event in the past which set everything up in full working order to be left to run on its own. If creation is a continuing process such language is meaningless. Special providence is thus more accurately regarded as part of the continuing creative act rather than as a distinct and subsequent action of a different kind.

But this is not the whole story. We are now in the post-evolutionary stage in which man is able, to some degree, to direct the course of evolution. On the negative side, this happens as a result of the exploitation of natural resources which affects the environment by endangering species and changing climate. Positively, man uses artificial selection for breeding purposes; his medicine and surgery ensure that the 'unfit' as well as the fit survive and we are now on the threshold of genetic engineering. Given that this is the kind of world which God intended one might expect it to be part of the plan that God and man should co-operate in the creative process. Paul's reference to us as 'fellow workers' (I Cor. 3.9), can be legitimately extended to include not only the evangelistic enterprise but also the evolutionary process. If God were not able to influence the course of events, in a sense he would be less than man who does have that power. The case for special providence is therefore a powerful one.

Moving on to the notion of miracle we come to something which is at even greater variance with the scientific view, though arguably less critical for Christian belief. The lives of many testify to the fact that a deep scepticism about miracles can be combined with a lively faith. Here we define a miracle as any event, directly attributable to God's action, which is contrary to the way in which the world normally works. In short it involves the breaking of a law of nature. As with special providence, the weakness of this definition is that it does not provide us with a sure test of whether a miracle has occurred. First, there are the obvious historical problems of determining exactly what happened. But the main, and insuperable, problem is that of knowing for certain whether, in fact, any law has been broken. Our knowledge of what these laws are is incomplete and it is always possible, however, remote it may seem, that the act brought into play other aspects of reality so far undiscovered. The transmission of pictures of Jupiter to Earth would have seemed a miracle only a few generations ago. In some cases, admittedly, the events reported lie so far beyond what now seems possible that one may feel confident in concluding that if the event happened at all, there could be no natural explanation for it. This would be true of the turning of water into wine. The distinctive ingredients of wine are simply not present in water and their creation inside water jars would require an incredible transformation of the elementary particles present. Raising from the dead raises problems of comparable magnitude. On the other hand many of the biblical healing miracles no longer strain our credulity even if the mechanisms are imperfectly understood. Even if miracles are not central to faith it is pertinent to ask whether they are necessarily ruled out in a world of chance. The broad issue of how God can act in a lawful universe is a longstanding one and we shall focus on the special features which emerge when it is discovered that much of the order arises from the aggregate properties of random events.

A spectrum of views

Before examining several of the major attempts to resolve the problem of chance and providence we set out some of the options available. Not surprisingly, Christian apologists have adopted a wide range of attitudes depending on the view they take of providence in general and chance in particular. The following is by no means an exhaustive list and some of the views are scarcely credible. They do, however, provide points of reference to which a more adequate view can be related.

Langford[3] describes three general ways in which chance and providence may be reconciled. According to one view God's action is located at the heart of matter where physicists have revealed a fundamental uncertainty principle. This is the point beyond which causal chains of events can be traced and no further. What appears to us, in our ignorance, as chance is, in reality, the guiding hand of God. A second view is that God does not act in (or on) matter at all but exerts his influence in the minds of people. Events in the world can therefore only be attributed to him at second hand. In order to achieve anything he must find a willing agent. The third view is not specifically religious at all. It is mainly assocated with the names of Jung and Pauli and more recently it was espoused by Koestler.[4] It is based on the idea of synchronicity, a so-called a-causal principle which accounts for significant coincidences by supposing that there are links of a non-causal kind which give 'meaning' to some coincidences. It is far from easy to see how a 'link' can be 'a-causal' or, even, how any meaning could be given to the notion. Even if we let this pass I cannot see how the idea offers any help either in locating God's action or in elucidating its mechanism. We shall therefore not pursue the matter further.

Another extreme view is rigidly deterministic in holding that every single event that occurs is pre-determined according to some master plan. Schoffeniels[5] seems to hold such a view though not on a religious basis. Muslim teaching also appears very close to this attitude. Determinism in this sense allows a belief in general providence – indeed it requires it – but special providence finds no place at all. If you believe that everything is governed by an iron rule of necessity it is hard to see how the Creator could intervene or why he should want to. In its extreme form this approach has little if any Christian support. From Thomas Aquinas onwards Christian apologists have seen the necessity of having some degree of indeterminism in the scheme of things if there is to be room for God to manoeuvre. St Thomas puts it thus:

> Now it would be inconsistent with divine providence if all things happened of necessity, as we proved above. Therefore it would also be inconsistent with divine providence if there were no luck or chance in the world.[6]

It is the fact that some choices remain open that allows both the possibility of divine action and human freedom. There is, however, a neo-deterministic view, having Calvinistic roots, which does have a measure of Christian support and is not so easily dismissed. This is that all happenings have their origin in the sovereign will of God. He alone is directly responsible for everything. According to this view the laws of nature are as they are because God wills it so and they remain that way only so long as he wills. In principle, they could be arbitrarily altered in an instant. The reason why this does not happen is because it is God's nature to be faithful. He wished his creatures to be able to rely on him. The fact that we live in a lawful world is therefore a reflection of the character of God, but he is under no necessity to behave in that way. Within this general approach there is room for variations allowing individuals a degree of autonomy and, perhaps, assigning independent power and freedom, at least in the short term, to the Devil. Nevertheless its characteristic attitude to chance is that summed up by the proverb 'The lots may be cast into the lap, but the issue depends wholly on the Lord' (Prov. 16.33). The uncertainty in the world is thus a reflection of our ignorance. Although we may be uncertain about what God is doing, he is not.

We have noted in Chapter 2 (p.24) that this approach is consistent with the scientific world view in the sense that nothing science could reveal could possibly falsify it. There is simply no need for a theology of chance since pure chance does not exist. Consequently there is no need to reconcile chance and providence. Everything which is logically possible and consistent with his character is within the power of God. If the occasion demands it he can depart from his mode of action and, for example, turn water into wine.

Although this view is self-consistent and in harmony with much biblical teaching it lacks credibility. Our claim here is that there is an alternative open to us which has equal biblical support but which does greater justice to the spirit of scientific enquiry. For this reason we shall not embark on a full evaluation and refutation of this philosophy. However, one observation is in order. The great strength of the neo-deterministic position is that it appears to take the highest possible view of God. It places no limit whatsoever on his ability to control and direct the whole universe. At the same time it is not obvious that such an all-embracing view of God is coherent. It may be objected that the sheer size of the administrative task of keeping track of what is going on in such an intricate universe as ours makes the picture of God controlling everything to be quite inconceivable. The obvious reply that this attitude merely shows that our minds are too small to comprehend God's greatness is not entirely convincing. For there seems to be a conflict between such a view of greatness and the idea of God as personal in the fullest sense. The more we make God seem like a vast computer keeping watch over everything, the more difficult it is to conceive of him as one capable of entering into close personal relationships with his creatures. The very idea of a personal God seems to require a focussing of his being which the 'cosmic manager' picture fails to capture. Most of these views deny that pure chance exists and hence there is no problem. The first, however, does treat chance seriously and we now turn to one of its chief exponents.

Pollard on chance and providence

The most sustained attempt to reconcile chance and providence was made by W. G. Pollard[7] in a book of that title. Having examined his argument one may well feel that his view is also essentially one of neo-determinism, but he starts, at least, from the recognition that chance occupies a fundamental place in modern physics. As a physicist and a theologian he strives to do justice to his experience in both fields. His approach falls squarely into the first of Langford's categories[8] since he believes that the springs of God's action in the world are to be found primarily, if not solely, at the sub-atomic level. His position is essentially the one set out earlier. At the heart of the atom we come to the point where causal explanation fails. If no other explanation for what happens can be found then, presumably, it must be attributed to God. Pollard allows that much of the uncertainty in the world is merely a reflection of our ignorance, but he maintains that when we reach the sub-atomic level, we find an irreducible randomness which defies all explanation in natural terms. He leaves open the question of whether there may be other locations of fundamental uncertainty in the biological or social spheres, and concentrates on the reconciliation of sub-atomic chaos with Christian providence. We now examine his argument in the light of the position reached in the last chapter.

Like Aquinas, Pollard recognized that, for providence to be at work in the world, at each juncture, there must be a real choice to be made about what happens next. If this were not so we should be back with determinism. Equally, it must be inherently impossible to predict with certainty which alternative will be selected at each juncture, since a God whose action is known in advance can hardly be said to be making free choices. God must therefore act, if he acts at all, at precisely those branch points at which the future is not predetermined. The events with which physics deals at the quantum level are of this kind and so where the scientist resorts to chance, the eye of faith will discern the hand of God.

At first sight there is much to commend this view which would probably be shared in some form or other by many Christian apologists. Langford points out that it can be criticized on the grounds that it is merely a sophisticated version of the 'God-of-the-gaps' fallacy according to which God is to be found at those points where science fails. No one who takes history seriously can feel secure in such a position since the advance of knowledge has a habit of closing those gaps and pushing God out of the picture. Like Langford, I believe that there is more to Pollard's position than this rather facile analysis allows. It would be premature at this stage to dismiss it as merely another manifestation of neo-determinism. We must first dig deeper. Broadly speaking there are two main strands to Pollard's treatment of uncertainty; they correspond to chance in science and chance in history. In this connection, like many others, he makes the useful distinction between chance and accident. The word chance is reserved for science and is virtually synonymous with what we earlier termed pure chance; accident is the term he uses in connection with historical events. It refers to 'situations in which two or more chains of events which have no causal connection with each other coincide in such a way as to decide the course of events. The accidental does not depend on the presence of choice and alternative as in natural phenomena. Two chains of events could each be rigorously determined within themselves and yet be such that their accidental convergence would decisively modify the course of history.'⁹ Accidents in that sense can also happen in the natural world but it will be an aid to clarity if we limit chance to the realm of science, and accident to history. We begin with chance.

Pollard points out that science is statistical in the sense that what is observed on the large scale is the aggregate of a multitude of happenings on the small scale. At the deepest level to which science has penetrated, we find a fundamental and impenetrable uncertainty expressed by the Heisenberg uncertainty principle. The fact of the matter is that at this level it is impossible to predict individual events because no causal mechanism is apparent. Unlike Einstein,¹⁰ who seems to have felt that there must be such a mechanism, Pollard is disposed to believe that here we have reached the boundary of knowledge. But since he also believes that 'the entire space-time universe is seen as a created affair, brought into being by a pure act of will of its divine Author, and ever since then the object, in its minutest detail, of his sustaining providence and mysterious purpose,'[11] it follows that these random events must be direct acts of God.

Science deals with repeatable events. Any individual outcome may be unpredictable, but a pattern does emerge when we look at large numbers of similar events. Thus, although we cannot predict when a particle will be emitted from a radio active atom, we can say that if a large number of particles is emitted the frequency distribution of the numbers in successive intervals of time will conform to a simple pattern known as Poisson's law.[12] By this means we can assign probabilities to individual outcomes, before we observe them, which correspond to these relative frequencies. Thus, although everything appears chaotic when viewed at the atomic level, simple patterns emerge when we move to a higher level of aggregation. The lawfulness of the world is then a consequence of the multitude of 'decisions' which God makes at the lowest level. God's 'laws' are thus to be seen, not in the events themselves, but in the probability distributions by which their aggregate effects are described.

If we accept this account the way is open to see how God can influence what happens in the world without needing to break his own laws. Since his laws are concerned with aggregate effects only, they do not say anything specific about individual outcomes. God does not, therefore, have to be seen as acting on the world from the outside but is at work at the very heart of matter. In the technical language of probability theory, God's master plan included the specification of the probability laws of all the random variables in the universe, but he left himself free to determine the individual outcomes as circumstances at the time required.

This account of chance and providence is attractive in that it provides a place for both without seeming to limit either. However, on closer examination a number of serious flaws become apparent.

In the first place it puts the cart before the horse in that it conceives of the probability laws being created first so that the events have to conform to them whereas, in reality, the reverse is the case. As Pollard sees it, God must have first decided on the laws and then, in some way endowed the events with propensities compatible with those laws. This seems to be based on a misconception about the nature of a probability law. In reality the laws are consequences, not causes, of the way things happen. Thus Poisson's law is the logical consequence of the more fundamental fact that a particle is no more likely to be emitted at one time than another. If we formalize this notion in a few simple postulates concerning equal chances and independence, then we can deduce that the relative frequencies will conform to Poisson's law. A great many of the statistical laws of nature are of this kind. They can be shown to be the result of simple random processes at a deeper level. They are not, in themselves, irreducible facts of nature. Such laws are not like those made by parliaments or clubs which have to be 'obeyed'. Rather they are simply descriptions of patterns in aggregate behaviour which are explicable in terms of underlying processes.

It can be maintained, of course, that this does not dispose of Pollard's argument, but merely shifts it one stage further back. It still has to be explained how it is that radio-active particles, for example, are no more likely to be emitted at some times than at others. However, what we often find, as in this case, is that what has to be explained is the absence of any particular pattern in the elementary processes. If it turned out that the intervals between successive emissions conformed to a simple law – say that the ratios of successive intervals were always prime numbers – then some explanation would be called for. We might well suspect that this fact was indicative of some deeper truth. But in our case there is nothing like this which cries out for explanation. The statistical laws seem rather to be consequences of the complete absence of pattern or purpose. The laws which were supposed to speak of the trustworthiness of God their author have thus dissolved in the underlying chaos.

A second point which has to be made about Pollard's argument is that it goes further than is really necessary. Since, in general, we are only interested in the aggregate effects of large numbers of micro-scopic events, it is not actually necessary to exercise detailed control over each particle. This was a central plank in the theology of chance which we attempted to construct in the last chapter. If it is sufficient to 'leave things to chance' why is it necessary to insist that such detailed control must be exercised? Put rather crudely, why should God bother with a host of details which do not ultimately matter? A partial answer is that some micro-events do matter and matter vitally. As Pollard notes:

> The phenomenon of gene mutation is the only one so far known in these sciences which produces gross macroscopic effects but seems to depend directly on changes in individual molecules which in turn are governed by the Heisenberg indeterminacy principle.[13]

Gene mutations play a vital part in determining the path along which life develops and here, surely, is the place above all where one would expect to find God acting providentially. The more recent work of Prigogine[14] and his colleagues also serves to emphasize and illustrate the important role which chance events play in facilitating the development of higher forms of molecular organization.

I have argued that even these critical events do not need to be directly controlled, but even if we allow the point, it is not necessary to go so far as Pollard in supposing that God is directly concerned with each single happening. A modified version of Pollard's argument would be that, although God is able to direct the course of every individual event, he does not, in fact, do so. He only intervenes on those rare occasions when it is necessary to bring about significant steps in the evolutionary process which nature, unaided, could not be relied upon to produce at the right time and place. This would go a long way towards the point of view advanced in the last chapter. The vast majority of events would not require any special direction and would be regarded as under the care of God's general providence. Special providence would be in evidence only on those rare occasions when something of crucial importance was at stake. Whether or not the miraculous could be accommodated within this view of things is not entirely clear. Although I do not find this a very plausible doctrine, it does largely avoid the third, and most serious, criticism of Pollard's account.

This is that the presumption that God is free to act as he pleases, subject only to the need to conform to his own probability laws, is not as straightforward as Pollard seems to suppose. The point at issue can be brought out by returning to a somewhat idealized and simplified version of the question of the sex ratio in human populations, already discussed in Chapter 2. For the sake of argument, suppose that the sex of a child is determined by pure chance and that all the births in a country can be unambiguously arranged in temporal order. The law, which God is presumed to keep in this instance says that, the sex of any child is female with probability one half independently of all other births. In the long run this leads to nearly equal numbers of males and females. Pollard would presumably argue that God is free to choose the sex of each child subject only to this long run requirement being met. Thus, although he makes a purposeful decision in each individual case, the aggregate effect is indistinguishable from chance. However, it is not sufficient that the proportion of females should be close to one half in the long run. It would not do, for example, to have male and female births alternating. Such a sequence would have no unpredictability and would be easily detectable as a serious deviation from what the law requires. In any sequence compatible with the law it must not be possible to predict successive members from knowledge of what has gone before. This means, for example, that whenever a male birth occurs it should be followed equally often by male or female. So if we take a large sample of male births and compute the proportion of them that were followed by a female birth that too should be close to one half. Continuing in this way any given pair of births, say (male, female), should be followed equally often by births of either sex. In fact no matter what sequence of births we may specify, the next succeeding birth must be male or female with equal frequency. Constructing a truly random sequence is therefore much more complicated than simply getting the overall proportions right. To be convinced of this, the reader may care to try to construct a series having the required properties. In fact the only certain way to ensure that the birth sequence was truly random would be to arrange that the need for children of each sex (to meet the wishes of parents, the demands of history etc!) was itself a random series. thus to keep one probability law, the divine author would have to create a second. It is now evident that we have taken the first step on an infinite regress in which an unlimited number of random sequences is required to achieve the object! This example is, of course, fanciful and rather contrived, but it illustrates the important fact that the idea that a large degree of freedom of action is consistent with conforming to a probability law is false.

If we return to the weaker version of Pollard's idea in which God only acts significantly on relatively rare occasions this objection does not apply. God's occasional interventions will then be lost in the mass of genuinely random events. If I toss a coin 1000 times and present you with the list of actual outcomes except in the case of the 171st toss where I give you an outcome which I had fixed in advance, there would be no detectable deviation from what would have been expected in a complete series of purely random tosses. Thus, provided that the proportion of occasions on which God chooses to act decisively is negligibly small, it will be impossible to detect his action by scientific means. We thus have a way of allowing room for God to work in the world without violating his own laws.

I doubt whether Pollard would allow that God only acts purpose-fully on rare occasions. He speaks of God acting in every individual case claiming that God is the direct cause of everything that happens. However, the apparent divergence need not be serious since we are at the point where special and general providence merge. There would be no inconsistency in maintaining that, in the vast majority of cases, the only immediate purpose in view is to achieve a local statistical balance whereas only rarely are the implications of a particular act more far-reaching. It seems more natural, nevertheless, to leave the great mass of events to chance, under the aegis of God's general providence, while reserving the rare and significant items for his special providence.

As we remarked earlier, Pollard leaves open the question of whether there might be sources of pure chance within the biological and social order which could also indicate the springs of God's action. He does, however, pay particular attention to the role of accident in the historical process and it is to this that we must now turn.

Accidents, we recall, were defined as events which occur as the result of the intersection in space and time of two or more causal chains (like those leading to the explosion in the coal mine, see p. 72). They can, therefore, be 'explained' in terms of antecedent events in the contributory causal chains. They cannot then be regarded as direct interventions on God's part; they must have been initiated by him farther back. Thus if his hand is to be seen at all we must trace the causal chains back to their origins in some fundamental random event at the sub-atomic level where all such chains begin. Let us agree to call such a point the 'root' of the chain. We must thus entertain the view of God manipulating events in history by orchestrating a number of such roots so that the causal chains which they set in motion intersect to produce the required effects. None of the resulting effects can properly be described as miraculous since they will all appear to be in accord with the natural laws.

By reducing accidents to products of the basic physical processes, we run up against the question again as to whether the need to conform to his own probability laws leaves God enough freedom to do as he wills. The difficulty now becomes more acute, since the production of a particular 'accident' may require the manipulation of a large number of roots and it is not clear that this number can be kept sufficiently small to avoid causing a more serious problem. In proceeding towards an 'accident' the contributory causal chains will intersect with many others all proceeding on their way to other intended accidents. At any one time there will then be a multitude of inter-weaving and inter-acting sequences sparking off accidents as they intersect. All of these accidents either have to have been 'designed' or foreseen to be harmless or, at least, tolerable. The complexity of the situation defies imagination. It is many orders of magnitude more complex than a game of chess in which not only must the end be foreseen, but also every event along the way. In view of all this it is far from clear that history can be adequately controlled by manipulation of happenings at the roots.

Since virtually all the alleged providential acts with which God is concerned have to do with historical happening, in the broadest sense, we may well be sceptical about the logical possibility of God doing things in the way that Pollard supposes. If it were possible then Pollard would be correct in his assertion that the reality of chance in nature and history is entirely compatible with the Christian understanding of God's providential care; it would also account for the fact that secular man can find no sign of the divine hand at work.

> If the laws built into the natural world really do permit through chance and accident many alternative courses for its history, as we Christians are convinced that they must, then secular man cannot by the very nature of things find anything within nature herself capable of removing this indeterminacy.[15]

The key word here is at the beginning of the quotation. It is a very big 'if' indeed. Pope made the same assertion more poetically in 'All chance direction which thou cans't not see'.[16] The case must remain unproven. Later we shall try to show that Pollard was looking in the wrong direction.

Pollard's case is not very far removed from that which we described earlier as neo-determinism. The common feature is that God is supposed to be in deliberate control of every single event in the cosmos. The difference appears to lie in the fact that Pollard believes that the statistical laws of physics were determined by God and that he is not free to depart from what he himself has willed. To this extent, therefore, he is not absolutely free. Neo-determinism finds it easier to accommodate miracles because then God is free to break his own laws.

A further problem posed by Pollard's solution to the chance and providence dilemma arises from another quarter. If God is orchestrating the whole of creation – including history – how can we assert that man is free in any real sense. This is the old problem of free-will and determinism but the question here is whether Pollard's general view makes it easier or more difficult to find a solution. Having asserted that all events at their root are divine acts, it is not clear how certain events resulting from human decision making can be said to be free – that is undetermined by God. If God's own providence extends to the whole of creation that must include human brains and hence to their thoughts and desires. Most of the providential acts reported in the Bible involve people. Were they merely puppets wholly under God's control, or were they free agents in any meaningful sense? By seeming to solve one problem Pollard has created another.

Pollard does not attempt to resolve the paradox of freedom and providence. Instead he points out that it pervades much of human experience and finds an analogy within physics itself. If in the most rigorous and exact of sciences we cannot escape paradox, then how can religion expect to fare any better? He cites the well-known fact that for some purposes the electron can be thought of as a particle and for others as a wave. Although it is an affront to common sense to speak of something as being two totally different things at the same time, the hard facts demand that we do the impossible. If this is necessary in physics, Pollard would argue, then it is not surprising that theology should contain a few seemingly irreconcilable elements.

This is an appealing and cogently argued view, and the Christian should not be unduly embarrassed by paradox. Nevertheless, if it should be possible to give an account of Providence which does violence neither to science nor doctrine, then this is clearly to be preferred. Paradox should be a stimulus to further search rather than an excuse for calling a halt. As we shall aim to show that such a reconciliation is indeed possible, there is no need to follow Pollard in the later chapters of his book in the attempt to tackle the problem.

Geach on chance and providence

Our second contribution comes from a philosopher, Peter Geach. In his book *Providence and Evil* he poses the question 'Is this seeming reign of chance compatible with Divine Providence?'[17] This comes at a point where attention has just been drawn to several well-known statistical regularities in which such things as the outbreak of wars exhibit a pattern entirely compatible with being the outcome of a lottery. Indeed the author uses Thackeray's description of God as 'The ordainer of the lottery' for the title of the chapter in question. Geach asserts the necessity of allowing a place for chance and comes down heavily against those Christians who think there is something improper about it. At the same time it is clear that he sees chance events as direct expressions of God's providence. The question just posed is thus answered by saying that God works through chance events. For Geach, like MacKay, Proverbs 16.33 is definitive. All events, however trivial, fall within the ordering of providence. 'But no detail of the universe is too petty for the Divine knowledge and will.'[18] This assertion echoes Pollard but is somewhat ambiguous. It is common to all Christian viewpoints that God is in some sense responsible for everything. What is at stake here is the extent to which each individual event is divinely directed to some identifiable end, rather than merely playing a contributory role in producing the aggregate effect of a large number of such happenings.

Geach claims that his view, as expressed above, makes it possible to reconcile chance and providence, but he allows that this does not make it a reasonable view of the way things are. However, he goes on to insist there is not even an apparent contradiction in affirming both.

A chance event is merely one without predetermined created causes, and there is nothing in this to put them outside the realm of God's knowledge and control. Geach then lines up with those who deny that everything is ultimately predictable, noting that this view is more common among scientists than philosophers. If everything is ultimately predictable there can be no real human freedom which is so vital to true Christianity.

Thus far Geach is in essential agreement with Pollard but he goes on to make three more penetrating points. He claims that the existence of statistical patterns of contingency does not exclude voluntary control of the course of events by God or man. One example is provided by the written word. Any substantial body of text will display statistical regularities. Sentence length distributions, relative frequencies of different words or letters and suchlike characterize an author's style to a degree which enables them to be used for helping to settle questions of disputed authorship. However, conformity to these probability laws does not constrain the writer in the matter of the truth or falsehood of what is written. A description of events, Geach claims, will display the same statistical character regardless of whether the subject is fact or fiction. One should, perhaps, question this assertion since style often does depend not only on the writer but on the subject and the intended readership. But allowing that to pass, the essential point is that meaning and form in language are almost, if not quite, independent. One can then alter the meaning without changing the overall statistical pattern. By analogy it is thus possible to conceive of God using this world of chance as a vehicle for expressing different purposes, without in any way violating his own probability laws. This is somewhat similar to the point we were making earlier on about sex determination. If the planned outcome for each birth is entirely independent of the temporal order of births, purpose will be neither detectable nor ruled out. As we have already argued, it is by no means obvious that this gives the deity sufficient flexibility, bearing in mind the large number of regularities implicit in a random process.

Geach's second point is that the single event can be manipulated without violating any long run frequencies. We have already noted this fact in the attempt to remove some of the objections to Pollard's solution.[19] As long as God only needs to intervene on rare occasions there is no conflict with the lawfulness of aggregate behaviour. But if only some events are specially controlled, it is not clear what weight is to be attached to his earlier emphatic assertion that 'no detail is too petty. . . . ' For if God is pictured as deliberating over every event why should there be need for special intervention, however rarely? If on the other hand God only acts deliberately on rare occasions while the rest, though in some sense under his general control, have no individual significance, Proverbs 16.33 is almost emptied of meaning.

The third point, which accords with the view which was emerging at the end of the last chapter, is that chance is a necessary part of the world if the supreme human dignity of individual freedom is to be exercised. Whatever the drawbacks may be, there could be no real freedom without chance (whether pure or artificial). To take part in the lottery is both necessary and desirable. In doing so we learn that God plays fair with us since though we can learn the rules of the lottery, we cannot change them. God's justice is thus expressed, in part, by the very indifference of creation – the rain falling on the just and the unjust again. This is not to say that every single thing that happens to us is a signal of approval or disapproval on God's part. What it does say is that none of us is singled out for special treatment of a favourable or unfavourable kind. If, however, what we call chance is the outcome of God's decision making, individual freedom requires that our free acts are excluded from this class of events. But if this is the case, it surely does not matter whether all external events are random or not. If man is free, he is free! If, on the other hand, he and his actions are to be considered as integral with the rest of creation and if all events in that sphere are directly or indirectly the acts of God, then he cannot be free. While I agree with the claim which Geach is making, it seems to me that it cannot be fully substantiated within his frame of reference. Later I shall aim to show that it can be justified within a framework which sees purpose primarily expressed in the aggregate effects of large numbers of genuinely random events.

Peacocke on models for God's action

In his Bampton lectures Peacocke[20] discusses how God can be conceived as acting in the world. His approach is somewhat different from that adopted by Pollard and Geach. In fact he confesses that he finds it hard to see what Pollard really means by Providence. Whereas Pollard was concerned with the precise location of God's activity, Peacocke does not appear to regard this as important. He leaves aside what happens at the heart of the atom and in the human consciousness, and seeks to explore the mode of God's action in the world of nature lying between these two extremes. According to him the probability laws which we use to describe the uncertainty in nature are descriptions of our ignorance rather than the expression of any fundamental or inherent uncertainty. This means that our failure to discern the causal links leading up to any event does not imply their absence. If such events really are linked, then there is no obvious place for God's action. Within the limits he sets himself, Peacocke seems to be disregarding the idea of pure chance and joining forces with Geach and MacKay.

Instead of attempting to describe the mechanism of God's action, Peacocke sets himself the more modest task of using models to give some insight into the way God might act. He is here using the scientist's idea of a model as an abstraction of the real world. Such a model is useful insofar as the relationships between the entities of the model reflect those which hold between the corresponding entities in the world. The use of physical models by engineers and architects is familiar enough. They are useful to the degree that they behave under simulated conditions like the real thing. Observations made in the model can then be used to infer the behaviour of the prototype. The model does not have to be an exact replica, in miniature; indeed it rarely is. It may be made of different materials and be devoid of all fitments which are not relevant to the aspect of performance under test. The important thing is that it is a sufficiently accurate reflection of reality for the purposes in mind. Models may not be physical at all. Often they will be mathematical equations or a verbal description of something already existing in the world which sufficiently resembles the thing under examination. All that is required is the facility to do things with the model, or to watch them happen, so as to obtain some insight into the nature of the real system. The use of models in this way is common in science and social science and is becoming increasingly common in theological discourse (see, especially *Myths, Models and Paradigms* by I. G. Barbour).[21]

Peacocke proposes two models for God's providential action in the world. His aim is to give some idea of how a transcendent God can be active within his creation. The first model which is also discussed by Langford, is provided by the mind/body relationship; the mind/body problem is to explain how actions stemming from the brain – which, presumably, is subject to the same physical laws which govern all matter – can express the will and intentions of autonomous self-conscious beings such as ourselves. The analogy here is obvious. In both cases a physical system is apparently associated with something much more intangible whose nature and mode of interaction with the physical system is real but unclear. The model here does not help us to understand how God might act in the world since we have little or no idea of how the model works. What it does do is to render the idea of providence plausible. For if a physical body can express the will of what we call mind, then it is not so difficult to conceive of a being such as God being able to express himself through the matter of his creation. Such a view is not new and it is subject to many difficulties, as Peacocke readily acknowledges. In its old form the model was unsatisfactory because it implied a duality of body and mind (the ghost in the machine), and hence of God and the world. Peacocke's reason for resurrecting the idea is that science now offers a new way of viewing these relationships. Thus consciousness can now be regarded as a property of highly organized matter which emerges at a certain level of sophistication but which is not fully explicable in terms of its constituent parts. Mind is not then something which resides in the body, or brain, but is a property of the brain itself but yet capable of initiating independent action and reflection (in the case of man, at least) on its own nature. In a similar way it is possible to imagine God as immanent and active in the creation.

This model is not successful, however, in safe-guarding God's transcendent character existing before and independent of his creation. God is not simply a property of creation which emerged at a particular stage of evolution. Peacocke acknowledges that progress has been made in meeting this criticism by process theologians who speak of God's relationship to the world in terms of panentheism. This term is intended to convey the fact that God exists in two respects – inside and outside of creation. This, of course, takes us beyond the model and so, in an attempt to remedy the deficiency, Peacocke proposes a further model.

He sees the trouble as part of a larger tendency to see God exclusively in masculine terms as a 'doer' actively operating on things and fashioning them to his desire. He therefore proposes a model in which the female aspect has more prominence. In particular he suggests that the growth of the baby in the womb suggests that God can, at the same time, be separate from and yet intimately connected with his creation. The child is wholly within but distinct from the mother and yet, in a vital sense, is part of her. So the world is distinct from God but wholly dependent on him and responsive to his will. Like all models this too has severe limitations. The child, for example, is of the same substance as the mother and, eventually will grow independently of her to the same stature and independence. The creation, on the other hand is certainly not a 'new generation' of God in the making. It is the relationship of inclusion of the one in the other which this particular model adds to the total picture.

Langford also assembles a range of other analogies, or models, which help to render the possibility of providential action credible. None of them gives, or is intended to give, help in understanding the 'mechanism' by which the Creator interacts with the world. But they help us to see why it is not so surprising that God should be able to influence the course of events. In this respect they differ from Pollard who, although he still cannot answer the ultimate question, at least directs us to the location of God's action.

None of these models is specifically concerned with the role of chance. Does the recognition that chance, pure or otherwise, is a basic feature of the universe pose any new problems? I shall argue shortly that we can and should go further, but the insights provided by these models are not essentially modified by bringing chance into the picture. They are a necessary part of the story but are not sufficient in themselves. If it had not been possible to provide such models, it would have been extremely difficult to make any kind of case for special providence. Now that that hurdle has been surmounted important questions remain. If everything is built on chaos, is God's hand only to be seen in certain significant rare events, as we hinted earlier, or can his purpose be expressed in any other fashion in the vast complex of processes conforming to probability laws? If God has a purpose, why should he appear to act so often in such an apparently purposeless way? We have already skirted around such questions but must now face them head on.

Providence in a world of chance

Let us first re-call the main elements of the theology of chance sketched in the last chapter and consider their implication for providence. We envisaged a God who had set in being a vast cosmos, rich with potential to produce intelligent beings capable of fellowship with their Creator. Chance was seen as part of the raw material of that creation accounting for the lawful behaviour of large aggregates, but also throwing up the enormous variety of living things for natural selection to work upon. That same variability provides an inherent capacity to adapt and develop which gives the biosphere a remarkable ability to regulate itself. Variety and uncertainty provide a stimulating and challenging environment giving full scope for human development as people use their intelligences to respond to the world in which they live. Although God was seen as ultimately responsible for every single detail, he was not regarded as personally directing every atom and particle to some pre-determined end. His purposes were rather to be seen in the aggregate properties of random processes. God chose to make a world of chance because it would have the properties necessary for producing beings fit for fellowship with himself. These beings are tested and tempered by the challenge of their environment until they pass by death into fuller fellowship with God. The individual is in a position rather like that of the solo pilot launched into the air for the first time. He is subject to all kinds of risks and his skills will develop as he responds to them. He can keep in touch with headquarters which may give him advice or instruction but are powerless to alter the weather or correct mechanical faults.

In order to focus the problem more sharply let us enumerate some of the things which one might expect a creative God to wish to do. In doing this we confine ourselves to the contemporary world leaving aside for the time being what might have been the case before the appearance of man.

If man is accepted as fellow labourer engaged in creative work, then a prime place for God's action would be at the springs of creative thought in the human mind. The provision of guidance, inspiration or whatever one calls the power which enables a man to rise above himself and bring new things into being, would then be an obvious expression of God's involvement. His special providence is then to be seen in all that creates the good, the true and the beautiful – in all the great works of science, art and literature.

Secondly, at a more mundane level he might wish to be involved in everyday decision making. Sometimes we make up our minds by ourselves, but many decisions are reached collectively. One person influences another by argument and gradually a common mind emerges. It is natural to see God as a party to decision making, influencing, but not making, decisions.

Just as God might collaborate with man, so it is possible that he might wish to oppose him if his actions threatened God's purposes in some vital way. Having given man freedom, the possibility is created that that freedom might be used to thwart his ultimate purposes. One might then expect God to be at work at those junctures where man makes mistakes, or threatens to. This need not extend to matters of detail thus destroying the uncertainty which, we have argued, is an essential part of nature. But it might be called into play in such world threatening matters as the pressing of the nuclear button.

Fourthly, if God has revealed himself to be a God of peace, harmony and wholeness we might expect him to be active on the side of reconciliation between warring factions, or in the alleviation of bodily suffering incurred as part of the price of living in an uncertain world. On this view God is seen as doing his best to mitigate the unpleasant features of the world which are necessary for wider purposes. This would find support in the ministry of Jesus.

Fifthly, it is conceivable that God might wish to demonstrate his power or his presence for some purpose. Just as the Shekinah cloud went before the Israelites (Num. 10.34) as a visible reminder that God was with them, so, in particularly difficult circumstances, there might be need for some act of communication of this kind.

Finally, and more doubtfully, since accidents play an important role in providing a challenging environment, God might wish to engineer coincidences in the manner implied by Pollard's view of chance and providence. In the light of the argument so far, this would have to be a very special circumstance in which 'unguided chance' had 'failed'. I think this brings us to the verge of contradiction but, since we have already noted that extremely rare perturbations of chance events are undetectable, they cannot be ruled out.

We now come to the nub of the matter. If God wishes to act for some or all of these purposes, how can he do it? Is such action inconceivable in a world of chance? We have, of course, already examined a number of approaches to this problem but, at the risk of some repetition, we set these on one side and begin from first principles. Few if any of the elements of our synthesis are new. What novelty there is lies in the way that they are fitted together in a theological scheme in which chance is regarded as real yet a part of the purpose of God.

We begin on a negative note by questioning an assumption which is implicit in much thinking and writing in this field and which is a barrier to a satisfactory resolution of the difficulties. It springs from the pre-eminence of physics in the hierarchy of the sciences and from its characteristic mode of working which involves explaining the higher forms of matter in terms of the lower. According to this way of looking at things the more we analyse matter into its constituent parts the nearer we come to the 'ultimate' explanation. Thus it was that Pollard's quest for providence led him to the sub-atomic world as the primary sphere of God's action. This reductionist approach to the search for providence is, I believe, mistaken. On the contrary, I would argue that it is at the opposite end of the scientific spectrum that we should expect to see the hand of God most clearly. The human mind, capable of reflective thought about its own nature and place in the scheme of things, is the most God-like thing we know. As we move from the building blocks of creation through the inanimate world to the more highly organized forms of matter which constitute the lower forms of life and so, beyond, to man, we are moving in a God-ward direction. Although the gap which still remains is enormous, the vantage point which man enjoys is the one from which God's action should be most clearly discernible.

The essence of this argument is that we are more likely to see the mind of God at work in the unpredictability of free human beings than in the unpredictability of sub-atomic particles. As has been noted before, an act cannot be directly attributed to God if it can be wholly explained as the inevitable consequence of antecedent events. There has to be a measure, at least, of irreducible indeterminacy. This, I maintain, is to be found at the roots of human decision-making as individuals exercise their inherent capacity for freedom of action. If God is able to exercise influence at this level, he thereby influences the course of events in the world.

This view is not without its own difficulties. It raises the serious problem posed by what is called 'double agency'.[22] If our actions can be controlled by an outside power, does that not nullify our own freedom? Or, how can the degree of responsibility for a given act be properly apportioned between God and the individual? If we speak in terms of 'control' and 'power' the difficulty is acute but it is much reduced if we substitute terms like 'persuasion' or 'influence'. This, of course, implies a degree of self-limitation on God's part by refusing to treat us as puppets. We can even allow that the strength of influence which God might seek to bring to bear might vary considerably from one occasion to another. It might be almost irresistible on some occasions, but man's freedom is preserved as long as it is not absolute. This harmonizes well with the view of process theologians who see God acting by persuasion rather than coercively.

The role of chance in this scenario is largely neutral. Chance is part of the sub-structure of reality on which mind plays. 'Mind' or 'spirit' responds to the kaleidoscopic patterns which the continual shuffling of nature throws up. Through his science and technology man acquires the power to affect the course of history and nature and so assumes a collective responsibility under God for what happens. Chance may thus determine what God in his providence is called upon to do, but it does not constrain his power to do it.

What we are advocating may be described as a 'top-down' approach to providence in which God is seen as exerting his direct influence at the highest level of creation. Pollard, in contrast, was describing a 'bottom-up' theology in which control was exercised from the lowest level. The 'bottom-up' approach has one very important shortcoming. As we have already noted, any attempt to control things from the lowest level must have regard to all the accidents which will be sparked off on the way to the intended end as the causal chain intersects with others. It is thus a very inefficient way of operating. By contrast, the 'top-down' approach is more precise and less potentially damaging in its unintended consequences. It is rather like treating a local skin condition by drugs taken in tablet form, or applied locally as an ointment. The tablet may effect a cure but also have a number of undesirable side effects. The ointment, on the other hand, may be able to cure the offending matter with minimal disturbance to the rest of the body.

The remaining question is whether God can act at an intermediate level – of stilling storms, turning water into wine or healing the sick – without any human involvement. Most miracles fall into this category and it is here that Peacocke's models are intended to help. The question is not how he does such things, but whether it is conceivable that he could. Although the body/mind relationship is perplexing, each of us has little doubt that what we will in our minds is translated into the movement of our limbs and our pens. Though this may seem incredible, it actually happens. It does not, therefore, seem too far-fetched to suppose that God is able to express his thoughts through matter in some analogous way. If this is allowed I believe that it is more fruitful to think of God as, in some sense, acting on matter rather than from within it. This avoids the need to explain how the apparent purposelessness of individual random movements could be the purposeful activity of God. Rather, I prefer to think of the basic randomness of the universe as the raw material on which God works fashioning into ever more complex and structured forms. We can lift a book from the floor on to a shelf. Without our intervention it would have remained on the floor, held there by the force of gravity. No law has been broken in defying gravity and raising it to the shelf. Other forces, over which the mind has control, have been brought into play which more than outweigh the gravitational pull. In much the same way it is possible to constrain the random movements of the molecules of a gas by confining it within a box. As a result, a new pattern of random movement within the box will become established. It is thus at least conceivable that God could directly arrange for forces of some kind which would direct physical systems in desired directions. There might be an analogy here with psychokinesis. If it is indeed true that the force of mind can affect, for example, the emission of particles from a radio-active source,[23] it is not beyond the bounds of possibility that the mind of God is capable of much greater things. This, of course, is highly speculative and rather less plausible than supposing that God's mode of action is by interaction with human minds. Nevertheless all we seek to establish is that the possibility of direct influence on the material world is not ruled out by acknowledging its random character.

Christians would claim that there is one supreme example of God's action in the world. This is expressed in the doctrine of the incarnation which asserts that God took human flesh and, in the person of Jesus, acted in the world. How this could be accomplished remains a mystery but, if the historical claim is granted, it illuminates the whole area. This idea of incarnation extends from that focal point throughout the life of the church, the body of Christ, and leads to a sacramental view of the whole of nature. The incarnation is the light by which we see the immanence of God in the world. In the dominical sacraments the elements of water, bread and wine are the instruments and signs of God's action, witnessing to his providential action throughout creation.

Where does this leave us? On the negative side I see too many difficulties in following Pollard in locating the springs of God's special providence at the sub-atomic level of matter. Although what goes on there is his responsibility, it is doubtful whether it is coherent to suppose that the world can be controlled from this level. Even if it were, it seems too cumbersome a way of doing it. Likewise I see no reason to go along with Geach and others who wish to attribute every single event in the universe to the direct will of God. He created random processes as a whole without it being necessary to plan the path of each element. Only thus, we may surmise could a universe of such richness and potential as ours be constructed. I see no reason to deny the possibility that, at least on rare occasions, God may take decisive action to direct the course of nature or history. At the same time I am disposed to think that the normal mode of his action is in the realm of mind. If God is primarily concerned with the creative thrust of his world, it is in the sphere of human creative endeavour that he is likely to be most conspicuously at work. If he is concerned with healing, reconciling and inspiring, his providence will be most fruitfully employed in the complex web of human interactions.

As to the precise mode of his action we can offer no adequate suggestion. I have emphasized that it is more important to establish that God could act in a world of chance than to discover how he does it. In Christian experience and theology the reality of the incarnation and the power of the indwelling Spirit express the vital principle that God does act.

According to the view developed in this and the previous chapter, chance is seen as grist for the providential mill rather than as an obstacle to providential action. To change the metaphor, the chaotic movement of elementary matter is the clay out of which the life of mind and spirit is fashioned. The picture is of an ever-creating God choosing to act in partnership with the very people who have emerged from the primeval chaos in realizing the potential inherent from the beginning. This is a majestic and worthy vision which both illuminates and challenges orthodox belief. It remains, in the final chapter, to explore some of these implications from a specifically Christian position. But this should not obscure the splendid vision of God who conceived a world built on chance and from which he continues to fashion something of eternal value.

7

Chance and Theology

From science to theology

In the last two chapters we have moved, increasingly, from the world of science to the world of faith. Unlike Pollard, who began from the position that his scientific knowledge and theological convictions must be accorded equal weight, we have made science the starting point. Only then have we sought to work out the theological consequences. The reason for proceeding in this direction, the reader may recall, was that truth is indivisible. Because the language of science is simpler and less ambiguous, we proposed to use the truth of science to illuminate the profounder world of faith and religious experience. So far, we have treated theology only in relation to the doctrines of creation and providence. It is now time to cast the net more widely by considering a number of other theological issues and asking whether the theology of chance accentuates or eases the task of the Christian apologist.

The transition from the scientific to the theological realm poses particular hazards for an author whose specialist knowledge falls within the boundaries of science. As an amateur in theology I must risk the stricture of those, like Julius Lipner, who consider that 'the attitude of the amateur theologian ought to command about as much respect as that of the amateur scientist or politician'.[1] Nevertheless, since few can aspire to equal expertise in both spheres, the risk must be taken. My only defence is that there is no harm in asking questions, especially within earshot of those who have the expertise to attempt answers. The aim of this chapter is not to make a serious contribution to theology but, by a mixture of questioning and speculation, to illuminate old problems from an unfamiliar angle in the hope of stimulating the interest of others.

I have aimed to show that the reality of chance is not merely compatible with the doctrine of creation but is required by it. This strong assertion is based on the claim that only in a world with real uncertainty can people grow into free responsible children of their heavenly father. But such a view, we argued in the last chapter, places limitations on the manner in which God can interact with that creation. It implied, for example, that the vast majority of events are not directly planned by God to achieve some immediate and specific end. We therefore had to formulate a doctrine of providence which, while allowing that God is ultimately responsible for everything that happens, did not require his intimate involvement in all things. Once we have opened the door to allow the occurrence of events not intended by God, questions are raised about other doctrines. Not that the introduction of chance necessarily makes the Christian apologist's task more difficult. On the contrary, it enhances the doctrine of man, goes a long way to reconciling undeserved suffering with the love of God, and emphasizes the role of the Holy Spirit. Even when it seems to undermine traditional teaching, as in some aspects of intercessory prayer, we shall argue that the loss is more apparent than real. No attempt is made to be exhaustive.

We begin with God. His role in creation and providence has been dealt with but the latter is closely bound up with his omnipotence and this needs further discussion. The way we regard God affects our view of man. God as Holy Spirit, indwelling and creative, fits well with the view that God works primarily in association with people, influencing rather than coercing them. A chancy world however, does raise serious questions about the incarnation – at least so far as it is to be regarded as essential in time, place and form. The Last Things have long been a source of puzzlement, and few Christians nowadays feel confident in making assertions about the End. Here, especially, one might hope for new insight into ancient truth.

Further reflections on the character of God

In traditional theology God's character is described in terms of such things as his omnipotence, his omniscience, his love and his righteousness. Any move which appears to erode his greatness, as measured by any of these attributes, is liable to raise serious doubts about the theological soundness of one's position. If God is God then surely there can be no limit to his power or knowledge or love. For this reason I have been at pains to emphasize at several points that such limitations as, for example, our view of providence seemed to impose, were not as serious as they appeared. Nevertheless, compared with the sovereign God of pure Calvinism, the God of chance may seem unworthy of the supreme status which Godhead implies. Have we then, in attempting to maintain that God is indeed the purposeful creator and author of providence, diminished him in respect of any of his other attributes? In particular, have we denied his omnipotence by claiming that some things happen which he does not directly intend?

The first point to make in reply is that we do not diminish God if we say that any limitations on his power or knowledge are of his own choosing. If he, in his wisdom, knows that his ultimate purposes will be achieved more effectively by allowing a measure of randomness in the world, then that is a mark of greatness rather than impotence. The second is that God is in no way diminished if he is unable to do mutually contradictory things. When we say that God cannot do something which it seems an all-powerful God ought to be able to do, we mean only that he has freely chosen that things shall be thus. He may have decided that he shall not be able to do something because it is not in his nature to want to do it.

The analogy of a parent and child is a helpful and familiar one. There are many occasions when the parent might wish to intervene in the child's play but refrains from doing so because a greater good is achieved by letting things take their course. A minor mishap now is much better than a serious accident later in life. The far-sighted parent who recognizes this is wiser than the one who considers only the immediate consequences. Geach proposes to use the term 'almighty'[2] rather than omnipotent to distinguish between a God who could do anything and one who chooses not to be able to do some things. It is rather difficult to base such a distinction on the etymology of the words but there certainly needs to be a terminological clarification.

We have argued that there are considerable benefits to be had from living in a random environment. God's power and knowledge is thus to be seen in his creation of such an environment. It would hardly be surprising if the best of all possible worlds, from God's point of view, seemed less than perfect to his short-sighted children. God's power has to be seen in the context of his wisdom. The former is only limited by the latter.

It is relevant at this point to say something about process theology. This seems to have much in common with the point of view presented here, especially as it relates to the omnipotence and omniscience of God, and it has been the subject of criticisms similar to those which are being anticipated here. Process theology sees the whole creation as 'in process' with God being immanent and transcendent. In his immanence he exerts influence (or pressure) and achieves things by persuasion rather than by edict. Time is seen as a real and essential part of creation with God responding to whatever happens in the universe; he is thus in a continual state of interaction with it. In a sense he shares in the struggle of life, suffers with his world and derives enjoyment from it. Thus in contrast to the impassable God of classical theology this God is very much involved with events and affected by them. It would be out of place here to discuss the merits of this approach, though, in passing, we note that it is by no means unbiblical. A useful introduction will be found in Cobb and Griffin.[3] Here we content ourselves with pointing out some of the similarities and differences in order to show how far the debate on process theology may be relevant to the points at issue here.

Superficially there is a strong resemblance between process theology and the modern scientific world view. Science views the cosmos as a vast random process. Out of the flux new forms arise, develop and, sometimes, disappear. The picture is one of a continuing process. It is a world rich in potential with many possible futures. Which path is taken depends on individual choices and the multitude of interacting causal paths. The chance and accident which are integral parts of this vast system ensure the variety necessary for advance. Process theology takes its name from the fact that it, too, sees the whole cosmos 'in process' of becoming. It originated with the mathematician and philosopher A. N. Whitehead and is essentially an abstract system of ideas to be judged primarily by its internal coherence and explanatory power rather than as a scientific model to explain the data of experience. Indeed, I can see no obvious point of contact between Whitehead's system and the practical world of science. Its hypotheses are not scientific hypotheses susceptible to experimental testing. It does, however, harmonize with the scientific approach in that it represents the world in dynamic terms.

One of the principal criticisms levelled against process theology is its doctrine of God and, especially, the problem it raises of reconciling his immanence and his transcendence. By making him so closely involved with the creation, it risks making him part of it. We have already seen how Peacocke dealt with a similar criticism in the discussion of the providence of God.[4] The limitation of God's power, which the process view seems to imply, is also very close to the difficulty we are facing here and it can be met in exactly the same way. More serious is the challenge of both views to omniscience. If God is somehow in time, does he know the future? If it is of the essence of things that the future is open so that we have real freedom, is not God limited in knowledge and power if he neither knows, for certain, what is going to happen nor has the power to do very much about it? In our case the problem is, perhaps, more easily dealt with. In the first place we have made no special claims about the nature of God's immanence. The problem of omniscience for us is how God can foresee all that is going to happen when the future depends on chance and accident and the free acts of individuals. There are two things to be said about this. The first depends on the distinction between determinism on the large scale and on the small scale. We have emphasized that chance at the level of the atom is consistent with law and predictability at a higher level of aggregation and, in much the same way, that individual freedom of action is compatible with 'laws' of social behaviour. It is thus possible to speak of knowing the broad pattern of the future and the ultimate end at the same time as insisting that chance is real. This would imply that God does not know every detail of the future but this in no way detracts from his greatness since these things are unknowable in principle. Such a limitation on God is a necessary consequence of his having made this kind of world. It would not have been so in a purely mechanistic universe if God had chosen that particular course.

The second thing to be said represents an alternative line of approach. This would say that God is also outside time and can therefore 'see' past, present and future and therefore knows everything. In his other aspect he is in time influencing the course of events. By this means we save omniscience in its most general form but at the price of leaving the relationship between God's transcendence and immanence unresolved. There seem to me more convincing grounds for arguing in favour of the first view, but there are difficulties in satisfactorily incorporating providence into it. For if God is active in influencing the course of events, without determining them, this must have been allowed for in his original calculations about the broad course which history would take – otherwise the final outcome could not have been pre-determined (if, indeed, it was). In other words, he would have to have been able to predict just how much influence he would exert without infringing man's freedom. This does not seem an unreasonable supposition.

In dealing with the apparent limitation which our theology places on God's omnipotence and omniscience, we have argued that God has as much power and knowledge as is possible, given that he decided to create this kind of world. We have not, so far, mentioned his other attributes and especially his love. A fair case could be made for arguing that there is no limit to God's love in a world of chance and freedom. That any increase in his power or his knowledge would limit the scope for expressing his love. It is obviously not so easy to feel and express love for a world of puppets as for one in which people are free to reject or return that love. A world in which there was no possibility of evil, in which we could not help being good, would provide no opportunity for the full potential of God's love to be realized. Without the powerlessness of the cross there could be no adequate measure of that love. It may be that there has to be some kind of 'trade-off' in which some of the divine attributes have to be restricted if others are to attain their full limits.

We also mentioned righteousness but there is little to add to our earlier remark that in a world of chance all are treated equally; there are no favourites – his sun shines on the just and the unjust. In the greater matters of judgment there seem to me to be no new problems raised, unless one were to argue that rewards and punishments had to be woven into the fabric of this present world.

Man

The view that we take of God has consequences for our view of man. If man were the pinnacle of creation designed in detail and carefully preserved as the child of God, his status would seem higher than if he were no more than an accidental by-product of the cosmic lottery. But this conclusion rests on a false distinction. I have argued that in spite of the indeterminacy of the evolutionary path, the end-product is very likely to be some form of intelligent life capable of reflecting on its own nature and influencing its own destiny. If this is so, we may infer that human life was what God intended and man remains his masterpiece. Mankind is no less the object of God's love for having come about in this way rather than another. But there is a further side to the question which did not emerge at the earlier stage of the argument. Although there seem to be good grounds for believing that a world such as ours would give rise to intelligent life, it was not clear whether or not the probability was sufficiently near to one. We noted that it was obviously not zero, else we would not be here to ask the question. This was sufficient to prove that the chance could be made as near one as desired by repeating the creative act as often as necessary. We did not point out that in ensuring that there would be at least one occurrence of life there would very likely be more than one. Would the appearance of (possibly) other forms of intelligent life elsewhere in this or other universes have any implications for the doctrine of man?

Scientists have debated the question of whether we are alone in the universe and there seems to be no clear consensus.[5] One school of thought argues that there is nothing very untypical about our solar system and that in a universe as large as ours there must be many other planets capable of supporting intelligent life. The other maintains that in the evolutionary chain there are so many points where things could go wrong that, even given the right initial conditions, the outcome we find on earth must be extremely rare. It would be surprising, therefore, if we were not alone. The argument set out above, which requires the chance of life appearing at least once to be large, tends to favour the former view.

It might seem that the larger God's family becomes the less he can care for each individual and hence the less significant each becomes. If God is conceived as having a finite supply of such care, the problem is already acute enough with the thousands of millions who have lived on this planet. More planets would make it even worse. On the other hand, such multiple families would add to God's creative achievement and so add to his majesty and greatness. Again we appear to be faced with a reduction in one attribute as we magnify another. However, there is no reason to suppose that God's ability to relate to individuals is limited in this manner. God is personal but more than a person and the mere multiplication of his children need not affect the status of any.

The Christian belief in life beyond death for some or all does not harmonize easily with the scientific world view. If life and conscious-ness are properties of highly organized matter, then one might expect disintegration to be accompanied by their disappearance. On the other hand, there are powerful images of death and resurrection based on processes in nature which can be used to support the contrary view. The introduction of chance does not seem to add much to the purely scientific debate on the matter. It does, however, bear upon one of the other traditional arguments for life after death. This rests on the appeal to God's justice. Since this world is manifestly unfair it is argued that a just God would require some other realm of existence in which wrongs could be righted. The force of this argument is weaker in a world under the total control of God than one which allows chance and accident. For if God is in full command, then he has the opportunity at least to see that the scales balance on this side of death. But if there are accidental blessings and misfortunes in this world, it is virtually certain that the account will not balance at the time of death. If God is to be just, he could only be so on a wider stage than this mortal life provides. God's existence and character must, of course, be established first but, once this is given, some form of immortality becomes necessary.

Other matters concerning man's status, for example, his sinful-ness and need for redemption do not appear to be affected either by the existence of many worlds or by the intrinsically uncertain nature of life in those worlds. There are, however, serious prob-lems about the idea of incarnation and redemption to which we turn next.

Incarnation and redemption

Christians believe that the man Jesus was unique in being both human and divine. In St Paul's words 'God was in Christ reconciling the world to himself' (II Cor. 5.19). The 'success', if we can so describe it, of the whole enterprise thus depended crucially on the work of Jesus being brought to its intended conclusion. If God's supreme intention was to reveal himself as love in human terms; and if that revelation was to be made at a particular place and a particular time so that people in all places and at all times might see and respond to him; and if it was necessary that his life should reach its climax in conflict with the Jewish establishment and result in crucifixion, then any serious disruption in the programme would have thwarted God's plan. But if the world is really as we have described it, then accidents will happen. If the details of the future are not under God's immediate control, then, as we noted in Chapter 5, he must have been taking some degree of risk in embarking on the incarnation. Suppose, for example, that Mary had miscarried or that the child Jesus had contracted a fatal illness; or that he had suffered a crippling injury in his father's workshop. We know that on one occasion at Nazareth the people sought to throw him over a cliff. If on that, or other occasions they had been successful, what would have been the implications for Christianity? Or again, suppose that Jesus had collapsed on the way to Golgotha with no Simon of Cyrene to step in and help. Could man's salvation have been wrought without the self-offering on the cross?

To many people, questions such as these will appear irreverent or, even blasphemous. The simple and orthodox answer is that none of these things could have happened because the whole life and ministry of Jesus was under the special providence of God. But this is too simple a view and, as a matter of fact, it strikes at the root of what it is designed to protect. There is certainly a degree of inevitability about the final stages of Jesus' life. From Caesarea Philippi, when he set his face to go to Jerusalem, the writing was on the wall. But a hundred mis-chances could have averted or diverted the final conflict. Indeed, there is much in the gospel record which hints that everything was not cut and dried. In the wilderness Jesus is tempted to throw himself down from the pinnacle of the temple. Was the devil right that no harm could possibly come to him? Or was the temptation real? Was Jesus facing the question of whether his father really did have that kind of control? The agony in the garden and the cry of dereliction are too genuine to allow the belief that the whole drama was a stage-managed affair in which the principal actor was secure in the knowledge that two days later all would be well. Unless Jesus thought that the crucifixion really could be avoided and that, in his last agony, he really did feel deserted, he was not truly experiencing the human condition with all its risks and dangers. To be fully human must involve being subject to all the chances of life. Yet, if this is so, we are faced with the conclusion that the plan of salvation could have miscarried.

It is, of course, possible to assert that, even in a world of chance, God's power is such that he could have ensured that the ministry of Jesus ran its appointed course. After all, his life was so special that an exception to God's normal mode of acting had to be made. We have already argued that very rare direct interventions would be consistent with the probability laws so there is no logical difficulty in saying that this is what must have happened. But in doing this we immediately return to the impasse we have been trying to avoid. If Jesus were subject to special protection, rather like a royal personage visiting Northern Ireland, then he could not fully experience in himself the human condition. The whole point of the incarnation would then be undermined by the partial denial of his human nature. Docetism would replace orthodoxy. Faced with this dilemma it is tempting to conclude that the world view we have adopted must be wrong. If things so vital as the incarnation and the crucifixion cannot be guaranteed, then the nature of things must be otherwise. Perhaps the Calvinist is right after all and God is directly responsible for every single thing, planning our lives in detail. But this raises even greater problems for freedom as we have noted before.

Notwithstanding the problems, there is much to be said for retaining the view that Jesus was no less subject to the chances and changes of the world than we are. It can be granted that Jesus had a better knowledge of things, especially of human nature, which would have given him a greater mastery over mind and nature than we have. He would thus be able to foresee hazards in time to divert them or use them constructively for his own purposes. His oneness with the Father and the wholeness of his personality would have freed him from some of the stresses and strains which beset the rest of us. He would have been immune to those diseases and conditions which are rooted in the mind. Since he lived life as it was intended to be, one would expect him to 'out-live' us in every respect.

But when all this has been said, even a perfect man could not be totally secure from accident or disease. Even if his parents were of the sturdiest stock, this would not be proof against a falling rock or fire. We repeat our earlier question. Could the redemption of mankind have been thwarted by some accident in the early life of Jesus? To some extent the answer depends on whether we believe that a particular sequence of events was essential. If there had been no Last Supper or no shedding of blood, would something vital have been missing? It is not difficult to allow that minor variations at least, could have occurred without affecting the main issue. In any case, the written records which we have are composite documents from various sources and they do not agree about all of the details. However, it is difficult to imagine anything like the Christianity we know without the central events of holy week. Even resurrection after a natural death would lose something of its force without the drama of the crucifixion.

In the foregoing discussion we have ignored one vital point. Jesus was not simply the victim of circumstances. He took charge of events and was partly, at least, in control. He set his face steadfastly to go to Jerusalem and after Gethsemane he did not flinch from the final conflict. But such a degree of control does not eliminate all risk and does nothing to deal with the situation which would have arisen if Jesus had never grown to manhood. In those circumstances what courses would have been open to God? Could he have made a second attempt if the first had failed? Was the successful attempt we celebrate the first? The fact that Jesus was apparently reluctant to claim that he was the Messiah might give some credence to the idea that his Father wished to keep all options open. But in resolving one difficulty we create a host of others, not least concerning the identity of two persons appearing at different times and places.

The simple answer that, in fact, none of these misfortunes did occur and therefore there is nothing to worry about, fails to grasp what is at stake. The question is 'could things have been different?' If so, the risk was real, and that raises the question of whether we can conceive of God taking risks.

There is one way, at least, in which one can imagine that all risk might have been eliminated without denying the reality of chance in the world. If it were the case that God could see into the future, even though he could act only in the present, one could envisage something on the following lines. Suppose that God contemplates an incarnation at a number of different places and times and is able to foresee the consequences of each such possibility. Might he then not choose one of those possibilities which runs its intended course? Whether or not it is coherent to suppose that what is not pre-determined can nevertheless be foreseen I do not know, but this line of thought raises another interesting question. Whatever view we take of God's providence in the world, we can only give meaning to the idea of incarnation if we suppose that the unique character of Jesus was a deliberate act of

God.[6] At what point then did his direct action end and natural processes take over? For example, was the sex of Jesus part of the divine plan or was it left to chance as it is for the rest of us? Does full humanity require exposure to this initial act of randomization or not? As Cressey[7] points out, the answer has far-reaching implications. It has to do with whether the maleness of Jesus was an essential part of his nature or an accidental feature. On this hang many of the arguments about the admission of women to the priesthood.

I do not have a satisfactory answer to these questions though it seems clear that the problems are no greater on the chance view of nature than on any other. I am inclined to think that the answer may be somewhat as follows.

Redemption like creation is a stupendous work. Just as creation called into play all the resources of an unlimited God, so redemption was no easy matter and not without risks. 'The fullness of the time' (Gal. 4.4 and Eph. 1.10: AV) I take to mean 'when everything was just right'. I imagine God choosing the time, the place and the manner of his supreme revelation in the most careful manner (though not necessarily with knowledge of all the consequences). The complete openness of the Son to the Father and their oneness with one another would have reduced the risks to a minimum, though not eliminated them altogether. All that was divinely and humanly possible was bent to the great end. But when all was done, things could have gone otherwise. It may be that there was no other way. It may be that God could, in any case, have turned a temporary defeat into ultimate triumph. We cannot know whether salvation history as it has occurred is what was originally intended. But none of this prevents us from grasping what is offered to us. Nothing in the theology of chance can take away what has been done. If the cost of love is measured in some degree by the seriousness of the risks that were run, our view of nature and history enhances rather than diminishes the victory of the cross.

The Holy Spirit

When we turn to the third person of the Trinity a rather different situation faces us. In many Christians' minds there is a good deal of vagueness about the nature of the Spirit often betrayed by referring to the Holy Spirit as 'it'. But in Pentecostalism, and among charismatics generally the Spirit often seems to dominate, if not exclude, the other persons of the Godhead. On neither view is the Spirit seen as having the kind of role to play that our treatment of providence or the history of nature requires. Rather than finding that the theology of chance threatens traditional beliefs, as seemed to be the case with the earlier topics of this chapter, we find here a failure even to make contact. This is not so, of course, if we turn to the work of biblical scholars. The Old Testament sees God as spirit active in creation, while the day of Pentecost marks his place in the church, working in the hearts and minds of believers. But he is not restricted to activity among believers. The New Testament also sees him at work in the world at large (as in John 16.8–11).

I maintain that the modern scientific understanding of the world, interpreted from a Christian point of view, requires a doctrine of the Spirit not essentially different from that of orthodox belief. Hitherto we have avoided the use of the term spirit, when speaking of God's interaction with creation in general and man in particular, to avoid religious overtones in what was intended to be a strictly scientific account. We have allowed the possibility that God might act directly on matter without the help of intermediaries, though such action would need to be limited by other considerations. For this purpose it does not appear to be necessary to endow matter with any 'spiritual' properties, though we did note a real problem about how such an interaction could take place. Nevertheless, the main avenue for God's action in the world was to be in collaboration with man. For this reason it is natural to suppose that there is something in the nature of man which gives him an affinity with God. Without claiming that words like mind, heart, spirit, soul, psyche or personality are synonyms, their existence testifies to the inadequacy of purely physical terms to encompass what we really are. Once we have allowed that there is a dimension of reality beyond the physical, it becomes meaningful to speak of God's interaction with man taking place in that realm. Henceforth, when we speak of the spirit of man, we are referring to that part of our total being which is nearest in character to God himself. His Spirit is the God-ward side of that relationship into which we enter in fellowship with him. If God is to have the means of influencing events, it seems plausible to see it taking place primarily at this higher end of the spectrum of creation. In this case, therefore, our theistic and scientific account of the world would be incomplete without some such view of God's all-pervading presence and activity. Such an idea is not unfamiliar in scientific thought. We are used there to the idea of fields of force whose influence is felt at all points yet are invisible and intangible. The analogy is, of course, incomplete because we do not think of fields of force as personal but it is useful in giving a way of thinking about the Spirit as both elusive yet real. The doctrine of the incarnation manifests the union of Spirit and matter in the person of Jesus Christ but, by its very nature, limited in location and period. The extension of that presence in time and space requires a doctrine of the Spirit. In the same way the action of God upon a world of chance requires a power and a presence unlimited by time and place. The two approaches harmonize and reinforce one another thus enriching our understanding of both.

Suffering and evil

The problem of undeserved suffering is one of the greatest burdens under which the Christian apologist labours. The situation is not greatly eased by the reflection that an earthly paradise would not be without its difficulties for the theologian. How a loving God on the Christian pattern could tolerate the suffering of his children, if he had the means to help, is a question not easy to answer. Even if God's existence be allowed, his apparent deficiency in this matter appears to undermine seriously his status as the supreme being. Does the fact that we have given a real and significant place to chance in the scheme of things make the apologists task any easier? I aim to show that it does.

First, we must insist that, as designer and creator, God is ultimately responsible for everything and hence for the fact that there is evil in the world. The baby too deformed to live, and the wasted figure of the starving refugee are thus both the handiwork of God in a certain sense. How then can he be described as good and loving with a desire for the well-being of his creation? Even if by some arithmetical artifice suffering and good could be added up on two sides of a celestial ledger with a balance struck in favour of good, the real issue would remain untouched. For why does there have to be evil at all? Some have been content to leave the matter in the realm of mystery and have sustained their hope by faith in the suffering Christ caught up in, and finally triumphing over, the cancer at the heart of his creation. It would be foolish to suppose that the matter can be satisfactorily dealt with by reason alone but that provides no grounds for not seeking for a rational explanation. Many reasons have been suggested to explain why a loving God might choose to create a world involving evil and suffering. Swinburne reviews many of them.[8] All but one of these (to which we return later) amount to saying with Leibniz that this is the best of all possible worlds. This is to be interpreted in the sense that if God had created some other kind of world, without evil and suffering, some vital principle would have been missing which would have thwarted the whole purpose of the exercise. The claim by dogmatic politicians that there is no alternative to their policies may well be received with scepticism. But the same claim on behalf of God may seem to belittle him by implying that his best was simply not good enough. Nevertheless, I maintain that the possibility must be taken seriously. It is impossible to prove that no improvement could have been possible. It would take the mind of God himself to encompass all the ramifications of such a proposition. What we may argue is that our view of the universe as a giant stochastic process makes it easier to see why such a claim might well be true. And, furthermore, it is one which not only explains the way things are, but makes them somewhat easier to live with.

We have argued that genuine randomness is a pre-condition of real human freedom and maturity and that because freedom is essential to that fuller life in God for which we are intended, then accidents could not be avoided. In such a universe the myriads of individual events which make up the kaleidoscope of nature and history must be in a constant state of unpredictable flux. Some of these events will inevitably work for man's ill and some, at least, will lead to events of catastrophic proportions. The random events which lead to mutation in the gene and hence to the advancement of life can also lead to deformity and suffering. There is an inevitability about suffering well express in Jesus' word 'Such things are bound to happen' (Mark 13.7, see also Matt. 18.7). The world view we have adopted allows us to maintain at one and the same time that God determines the end and the lawfulness of the macro-universe and that there is indeterminism on the micro-scale. We do not then have to attribute the ravages of a bacterium or the eruption of a volcano to his deliberate purpose. At the risk of labouring the obvious, we repeat that the problem of evil would be almost insuperable in a deterministic world since then God would be directly responsible for everything, though even then it might be possible to argue that there was no better way. Our view, however, allows a genuinely creative role to man as the fellow-labourer and fellow-sufferer with God.

Not only does this general viewpoint indicate why evil may be a necessary, though transitory, part of creation but it also offers real comfort to the sufferer. It is all very well, the critic may argue, to pontificate about the inevitability of suffering from an academic armchair. It is another matter entirely when evil has to be confronted in the flesh. That a law of averages requires that some shall suffer is small comfort to the one who suffers. True though this is, suffering can be aggravated by the belief that it has been deliberately inflicted. The bitterness against God sometimes shown by those who feel that he is to blame for their suffering only serves to deepen the pain. It warps the personality and helps to destroy both body and spirit. As Jesus said to the Pharisees 'It is not that this man or his parents sinned' (John 9.3). This is not to say that suffering could not be used by God to chasten an individual, but that in the normal course it is not so used. The sufferer is thus relieved of the burden of guilt that has been unnecessarily placed on his shoulders. He can be assured that he has not been singled out and is not necessarily more deserving of punishment than anyone else. Like the rain, pestilence and disaster fall on the just and unjust alike. Illness and injury must therefore be taken as part of life, but with thankfulness that, through the care and skill of others, in many cases the suffering can be relieved. Even if death results, God's care extends beyond the limits of time to a sphere where love is supreme and where suffering is no more.

Of course, the problem has been overstated. We do not have to justify suffering which is caused by the carelessness and folly of others. The person who is paralysed as a result of crashing his motor cycle while drunk is not the victim of uncertainty in the world. There is no doubt that the world's burden of suffering is much greater than the economy of God's creation calls for. It is partly and, sometimes almost entirely, a product of the evil within ourselves and others. It is much easier to explain why God might fail to restrain the wickedness of people than to justify suffering which can be laid at no one's door.

I mentioned at the beginning of this section that all but one of the explanations for the existence of evil mentioned by Swinburne rested on the belief that there was no better way. The exception is the traditional view that evil is the work of a fallen angel (or angels) in rebellion against God.[9] If this is so, many of the difficulties disappear. If there are other agents at work besides ourselves and God, his character is saved by attributing all unloving acts to devils. But in removing one set of problems we introduce others. Even if we leave aside the question of the existence of such creatures, we still have to explain how they can interact with people and nature. It is the problem of God's providence in reverse – a kind of anti-providence. Influence at the level of mind is no less plausible in the case of devils than in the case of God or other people. But it is natural disasters of flood, earthquake and hurricane that pose the greatest challenge to belief in the love of God. We saw difficulty enough in understanding how God could intervene on anything but a small scale in the workings of natural processes, without disturbing the natural laws which testify to his faithfulness. It is certainly no easier to allow such powers to lesser beings though it obviously cannot be ruled out. However, there is a more serious objection to this line of explanation. It erodes, if not eliminates, the place of pure chance in the scheme of things. By attributing to purposeful beings 'accidental' events which cause suffering we are removing such events from the sphere of chance. This undermines our central argument that chance is real and intended by God. The picture becomes one in which the all-powerful God of neo-determinism is replaced by a committee with conflicting interests but collectively having direct control of everything that happens. Both alternatives are equally inimical to the scientific world view.

Prayer

Prayer involves communication between God and man. It has many aspects. In the popular mind it is seen primarily as a way of getting God to do things for us. Though the Christian will rightly protest that there is much more to prayer than this, it is intercessory or petitionary prayer that raises the problems. There is little point in asking for anything unless we are reasonably assured that the one who is asked has the power to grant the request – or, at least, to exert some influence in the desired direction. Yet we have seriously questioned whether this is the kind of world in which God, even if he were willing, would be able to bring about the sort of changes that are sometimes requested.

Prayer is, of course, two-way communication and this implies that God may also make requests of us. This is often overlooked and it is worth emphasizing if only to point out that in this direction, at least, the world of chance poses no real problems. Granted that we have a measure of freedom to act as we please we are free to respond to God's prompting and to do what he wills. Prayer has then achieved something. Religious history, from Abraham onwards, is full of examples in which individuals have believed that God was speaking to them. From Moses to Joan of Arc and Billy Graham great events have turned on what was believed by the recipient to be direct communication from God. Many humbler vocations have been similarly determined. Although this is an area where delusion and deception are rife there remains a substantial residuum of cases where divine guidance is claimed with some plausibility.

But the real problem lies with traffic in the opposite direction. There are, of course, many reasons why God might not answer prayer, even if he had the power to do so. He obviously could not simultaneously satisfy petitions with contradictory desires. Neither could he be expected to do things contrary to his nature or to the longer term benefit of his will for the petitioner. The Christian devotional literature is rich in wise counsel for those who have unreasonable hopes and expectations in this direction. Nevertheless, we have supposed that God has, by his own choice, created a world in which accidents happen and hence in which there is bound to be distress and suffering. Is it not then reasonable to expect him to remedy the situation when this can be done without interfering with his overall purpose? But even if this is granted it has to be explained why an all-seeing God needs to have these deficiencies pointed out to him. One answer is that God has chosen to give man responsibility and to make him a partner in the work of continuing creation. Just as the child learns the parents' wishes by asking questions, so we, by observing which of our requests are granted, will learn the way God wants things to go. This proposition requires much deeper analysis, but all we seek to show here is that it is not unreasonable that we should make requests to God with a reasonable expectation that he will hear and answer them on some occasions, at least. The question then is one of whether it is possible for God to respond and hence of whether it is worth our while to ask.

For convenience, let us divide requests into two main classes each with two divisions. The first class consists of those requests which involve making some adjustment to physical processes. These may be subdivided into those which appear to be in harmony with natural laws and those which are not. Praying that it might rain sometime during the next week would belong to the first category, but praying that it would rain forthwith from a clear blue sky would be in the second. This example illustrates how difficult it might be to distinguish clearly the two cases as there is a range of possible requests between these two extremes. The second main class concerns prayer directed at affecting persons; these too may be divided into those which appear miraculous and those which do not. A request that someone might change their mind would not (usually!) be considered miraculous whereas a request that sight might be restored to an eye whose optic nerve was severed certainly would. (It could be argued that this last example belongs in the first class since it seems to require a physical construction to overcome the problem. But since the relationship between mind and body is so obscure it seems more sensible to allow that such 'miracles' might be achieved through the agency of mind.)

There is nothing essentially new here since we have already dealt with such matters, in principle, under 'Chance and Providence'. The only novel feature when we turn to prayer lies in the matter of asking and being heard. Our ability to communicate with God operates in the realm of the spirit and hence is not obviously affected by the nature of the physical processes in the world. Whether or not intercessory prayer is worthwhile, therefore, turns on God's ability and willingness to respond. It is worth making a brief recapitulation of our earlier conclusions in order to relate them to the typical subject matter of prayer.

Action in the physical world might originate at one of two levels. One is in the sub-atomic realm which was where Pollard supposed that God acted. We have argued that even though action at this level could not be ruled out it seemed an indirect and very complicated way of working. Even allowing the possibility it is not easy to imagine how a bullet could be diverted in flight or a poison be rendered harmless, to mention only two evil outcomes which one might wish to avert. The second mode would involve some form of 'pressure' on physical processes designed to steer them in desired directions. There is an analogy here with the way in which we direct the course of events, for example, by building dams or making speeches. An idea in our mind is converted into a tangible change in the world through the agency of our bodies and those of others. If a full explanation of how this happens is lacking, we cannot expect to comprehend how God might achieve his purposes. The weakness of the analogy is that God does not have a physical body through which to work. Nevertheless, if God does have some means of directing physical processes there is nothing irrational about praying that he will do so. The fact that many such processes are the aggregate effect of many essentially random happenings is neither here nor there. By deforming an inflated balloon we are merely altering the boundaries of the region within which the randomly moving molecules are constrained to move. Once more we see how useful it is to think of randomness as a kind of 'raw material' which can be moulded into shape by external forces.

However this may be, it seems clear to me that it is in the realm of mind that God should be seen as primarily at work. There are, as we have noted, problems in conceiving how this interaction takes place and what is the nature of the dimension of reality which we designate as spirit. But given that it does so take place, there is no fundamental difficulty posed by the universe of chance. For action resulting from prayer will be by means of human agency. In large measure this will be within the realm of ordinary human activity and so would occasion no surprise. Some things, it is true, do appear to be beyond the normal powers of human beings and therefore to be, in a sense, direct acts of God. Examples are provided by some cases of divine healing where apparently irreversible physical damage is repaired. Here, God is not to be seen as influencing someone to do something which, in principle, they could have done of their own volition; rather he is using the healer as a channel or a tool for the display of divine power. Does the stochastic basis of physical processes render this more or less credible? In so far as a stochastic system is more flexible and malleable than a rigidly mechanical system, it is possible that it is more susceptible to 'pressure' by external influences of divine origin.

Radical rearrangements of molecular structure may be less inconceivable within this framework than in one which is excessively 'lawful'. I do not pretend that it is easy to explain these matters, but it is sufficient for our purposes that, if anything, the new world view makes the efficacy of prayer rather easier to believe in than the deterministic alternative.

There are two further points I would wish to add. One is that, whatever some Christian apologists may say, most intercessory prayer that is actually offered is directed at achieving something within the minds of other people. If one examines the petitions in the service books of the main Christian bodies, the diaries of private prayer, or listens to prayers of any kind, hardly any are directed at producing direct physical changes.[10] The liturgies are almost entirely concerned with the world of people – the church, friends, neighbours, governments and those in special need. Such prayers, if answered, would effect significant changes in the way people feel and act or in their health and well-being. An excellent example is provided by the Lord's Prayer which provides the model for so much private, as well as public, prayer. This is almost entirely concerned with people and their relationships. The only possible exception, noted in Chapter 6, is 'give us today our daily bread' (Matt. 6.11 and Luke 11.3). But few, in uttering these words, expect it to be handed to them on a plate! We depend on other people for our food as much as on the climate both in the long and short term. It could be argued that this is an indirect request for good growing weather and hence for a physical act, but the case is at best an indirect one.

The second point is that, to some, most of the foregoing discussion will seem superfluous. How God might be able to answer prayer pales into insignificance beside their conviction that he does. There are, indeed, many remarkable instances on record of what seem to be direct and clear-cut answers to prayer. To suggest that these happenings were merely coincidences is scarcely credible to those who have been involved. Yet the point has to be made that the divine connection can never be proved. It is an elementary logical fallacy to suppose that because B follows A in time it is directly caused by A. The nearest we can come to establishing causality is by controlled experiment and this, in the nature of the case, is impossible with prayer – you cannot experiment with God. In a world of chance it is inevitable that coincidences will happen. In order to prove the efficacy of prayer by scientific means it is not then sufficient to demonstrate that the event prayed for came to pass. It would also be necessary to show that, in a large number of such praying situations, the number of such 'answers' occurred significantly more frequently than would be expected in the absence of divine action. The position is essentially the same as in the case of extrasensory perception discussed in Chapter 5 (p. 115). The task is made harder by the fact that it is very difficult to know how to calculate how many apparent answers to prayer would occur if God did not answer prayer. Perhaps the most we can expect to do on the scientific plane is to show that God is not precluded from answering prayer by the character of the world he has made.

The Last Things

Traditional Christianity teaches that the whole of history is moving to a grand climax in which all things will be summed up in Christ. The ways in which this culmination is pictured are very varied so that any attempt to see whether faith and science are compatible in this area must reckon with a whole spectrum of views. At one extreme are those who, following the imagery of the epistle to the Thessalonians, expect the trumpet to sound and true believers to be caught up in the air to meet their returning Lord (I Thess. 4.16, 17 and II Thess. 1.7). Others, nearer the other extreme, would say that the promised second advent occurred at Pentecost with the coming of the Spirit. Such a view may or may not be associated with a belief in some future event winding up history with a 'day of judgment'. Most, if not all, views of the Last Things would include the triumph of good over evil at the completion of the battle whose victory over sin and death is already foreshadowed on the cross. Less traditional, but in harmony with the general religious outlook, is the view of Teilhard de Chardin who saw the whole creation moving to a culmination in what he termed the omega-point.[11]

In so far as these views envisage an intervention from outside the system, they are neutral as regards the theological perspective which we have been exploring. It is true that the aerodynamic and physiological problems associated with a large influx of angelic hosts into the upper atmosphere would not be easily explicable in conventional scientific terms. Neither would the more fundamental questions of how such visible personages could materialize out of nothing in the depths of space be easily answered. The view that one would take on such matters would obviously depend on one's attitude to miracles generally. This has already been discussed and we shall not repeat the arguments here.

I prefer to treat the matter somewhat differently and in two parts. The first concerns the question of whether it is conceivable, in view of our scientific knowledge, that God could control the historical process in such a manner as to lead to an 'end of the world situation' such as is suggested in many New Testament passages. A closely related question is whether such control is actually necessary, or whether the projected end is virtually certain in any case.

The second part has to do with whether the uncertainties inherent in the physical universe or the consequences of man's free acts could wreck God's intentions or thwart his attempts to rectify matters. At the physical level it is conceivable that some physical catastrophe might destroy life. (As remarked in Chapter 2 there appears to be some evidence that giant meteorites did collide with the earth in the distant past though the impacts were not sufficient to destroy all life.) An obvious Christian response to this possibility would either be to say that God could foresee the impending collision and so would adjust the orbits in question before any harm occurred, or that God, who foresees all eventualities, would not have designed a universe in which such things could happen; his creation is too precious to expose to such risks. The second example is on the human level. Mankind now possesses the power to obliterate civilization. This could be deliberate or accidental. 'Accidental' here covers a multitude of human actions or mis-calculations. Again, the simple answer would be that God would intervene, probably in the minds of potential perpetrators, to divert the intention which, if carried out, would lead to annihilation. This, of course is always supposing that it is not God's will that the end should be ushered in with a nuclear holocaust from which the faithful would somehow be rescued. Such an event would be a fair representation of Armageddon as pictured in the book of Revelation.

What are the less simplistic interpretations open to the Christian? We begin by acknowledging that any doctrine of the Last Things must reckon with the scientific fact that life on earth cannot go on for ever. The dissipation of energy from the sun will eventually lead to the death of all life even if no catastrophic event cuts it short. Starting from this, the Christian has to explain how the fruits of creation which have lasting value are to be preserved for eternity. Will the angel reaper be for ever at work until time is no more, or will God engineer or wait for (if that is necessary) a consummation in some special manner at the end. I think it is unprofitable to enter into speculation as to the scientific feasibility of the various eschatological scenarios which have been constructed from biblical materials. Instead, I shall suggest some general lines of thought which arise out of the scientific world view and which harmonize with a reasonable interpretation of the biblical story.

On the physical level of nature we must accept the real possibility of physical disaster whether by celestial collision, deadly disease, famine or climatic variation. Given the size of the universe and the very narrow range of conditions under which human life can emerge and flourish it may well be that the chance of such a disaster occurring during human history is so minute that it can be ignored. But if the worst did happen, one would expect God to have a contingency plan for repairing the damage either in this world or the next. I reject the idea of a physical intervention to avert disaster on the grounds that this idea does violence to the orderly pattern of the universe and would thus be contrary to the character of God as we know it. The view that such happenings are impossible because God would not have designed such a universe is not tenable within a world where chance is real. The difficulties which the physical risks pose *a priori* are, of course, much diminished by the fact that such a disaster did not happen before civilization developed to the point where mankind assumed some degree of power over its own destiny. *A posteriori*, therefore, there is no practical problem. If God was really taking a chance, it has 'come off'. If not, there is no problem.

The more substantial question concerns the course of history. We have argued that, whatever power God may exercise directly, a main arena for his action is in the realm of mind. To a substantial degree, the course of history is determined by what goes on in people's minds. God, who sees all, could therefore be expected to know what was in the heart of man and to exert influence or pressure at critical junctures to keep history broadly on course. When man was limited in the damage he could do to his fellows or his environment, it would be possible to cope with even quite major mishaps by this means. Civilization has already suffered plague, famine and warfare on a massive scale but, always, the resilience inherent in creation has been sufficient for recovery to take place. In these circumstance it would be plausible to argue that God could exert sufficient control or even, that the great stochastic process of nature and history was heading for a pre-determined end without his needing to bother. Now things have changed. A single error or mis-calculation on the part of one individual could set in train events which would destroy or mutilate all life on earth. The chance of such an error (setting aside the possibility of destruction being deliberately set in motion) is clearly not zero. Without disarmament, the probability of disaster occurring within a century or so must be quite high. It is still possible to maintain that God could prevent such a disaster by bringing sufficient pressure to bear on key individuals, but this argument could not be invoked for mechanical or electronic error.

One possible scenario is as follows. It was inherent in creation from the beginning that people would abuse their freedom and that conflict would be endemic in society. It was also inevitable that as knowledge advanced and as more power accrued to man the scale of conflict would increase. And this in spite of the message of the Prince of Peace and his followers. The signs of the end foretold by Jesus are thus to be seen as no more than a true reading of the character of human life and history. Whether or not particular utterances actually related to events like the destruction of Jerusalem in AD 70 or to some greater cosmic event is not the main point. What counts is that the nature of the world and its inhabitants is such that sooner or later life as we know it would probably be wiped out. With this possibility in view, God would have to demonstrate that the ultimate triumph of evil was only apparent. Just as the good in human civilization might one day be destroyed, so the perfect man met destruction on the cross. To Christians the resurrection is the sign of where the ultimate truth lies. The divine plan thus has to provide for the establishment of a new order beyond death and destruction into which all that is of lasting value is incorporated. The earth, having served its purpose, can then be left to its fate.

None of this requires God to interfere with natural processes or to 'over-rule' the intentions of wicked men. But neither does it rule out the possibility of his influencing or, even, determining the course of events at certain critical junctures. Even if disaster is virtually certain sooner or later, God may well wish to influence, if not control, the course of events on the way to that end. What matters to the Christian is that what ultimately counts is not subject to the changes and chances of this fleeting world.

NOTES

1. *God and Chance*

1. Jacques Monod, *Chance and Necessity*, Collins 1972. English translation of *Le hasard et la nécessité*, Seuil, Paris 1970.

2. Fred Hoyle and Chandra Wickramasinghe, *Evolution from Space*, Dent 1981.

3. This is a collection of Aristotle's writings put together in the late middle ages.

4. See, for example, R. Hooykaas, *Religion and the Rise of Modern Science*, Scottish Academic Press 1972; new edition with corrections 1973. See especially p. 13.

5. The full quotation taken from Ronald W. Clark, *Einstein, the Life and Times*, Hodder & Stoughton 1973, p. 48 is: 'An intelligence knowing, at a given instance of time, all forces acting in nature, as well as the momentary position of all things of which the universe consists, would be able to comprehend the motions of the largest bodies of the world and those of the lightest atoms in one single formula, provided his intellect were sufficiently powerful to subject all data to analysis; to him nothing would be uncertain, both past and future would be present in his eyes.'

6. Clark, op. cit., p. 327.

7. William G. Pollard, *Chance and Providence*, Scribner, New York 1958, Faber & Faber 1959.

8. Monod, op. cit.

9. Pierre Teilhard de Chardin, *The Phenomenon of Man*, Collins 1955.

10. J. Lewis (ed.), *Beyond Chance and Necessity*, Garnstone Press 1974; Teilhard Centre for the Future of Man 1976.

11. Ibid., p. 12.

12. Adolphe Quetelet, *Essai de Physique Sociale* (2 vols), Bachalier, Paris 1835 (2nd ed. 1869). The term *social physics* seems to have originated with Auguste Comte who later abandoned it for *sociology* to avoid confusion with Quetelet's statistical science. (See Peter Halfpenny, *Positivism and Sociology*, Allen & Unwin 1982, pp. 14 and 32.)

13. Adolphe Quetelet, *Letters on the Theory of Probabilities as Applied to the Moral and Political Sciences* (translated from the French by O. G. Downes) C. and E. Layton, London 1849. Prince Albert evidently learnt his lessons well; he referred to the problem of reconciling statistical law and religion in his presidential address to the International Statistical Congress in 1860. (*Journal of the Royal Statistical Society*, 23, pp. 277–285.)

14. An account of Florence Nightingale's views will be found in Marion Diamond and Mervyn Stone, 'Nightingale on Quetelet I', *Journal of the Royal*

Statistical Society, Series A, 144, 1981, pp. 66–79. The article is continued on pp. 176–213 and 332–351.

15. Herbert Butterfield, *Christianity and History*, G. Bell and Sons 1949; Fontana 1957. The quotation is from pp. 123f. of the latter.

16. Joseph Conrad, *Chance: A Tale in Two Parts*, Dent 1913, Collected Edition, 1949. Author's Note.

17. Ibid., pp. 99f.

18. James Hilton, *Random Harvest*, Macmillan 1941.

19. Arthur S. Peake, *The Nature of Scripture*, Hodder & Stoughton 1922, p. 237.

2. Chance and Necessity

1. Jacques Monod, *Chance and Necessity*, Collins 1972.

2. From a conversation recorded in June 1972 and broadcast on BBC 3.

3. Monod, op. cit., p. 110.

4. James D. Watson, *The Double Helix*, Weidenfeld & Nicolson 1968.

5. C. H. Waddington, 'How Much is Evolution affected by Chance and Necessity?', *Beyond Chance and Necessity*, ed. J. Lewis, Garnstone Press 1974, pp. 89–102.

6. R. E. Monro, 'Interpreting Molecular Biology', *Beyond Chance and Necessity*, pp. 103–120.

7. Stephen J. Gould, 'The Chance that Shapes our End', *New Scientist*, 5, February 1981, pp. 347–349.

8. Digby McLaren, 'Impacts that Changed the Course of Evolution', *New Scientist*, 24, November 1983, pp. 588–593.

9. J. Lewis, 'The Cartesian Paradox', *Beyond Chance and Necessity*, pp. 27–50.

10. E. Schoffeniels, *Anti-Chance*, Pergamon Press 1976, translated from the second edition of *L'Anti-Hasard*, Gauthier-Villars, first edition 1973.

11. Donald M. MacKay, *Science, Chance and Providence*, Oxford University Press 1978.

12. A. R. Peacocke, *Creation and the World of Science*, Clarendon Press 1979.

13. Donald M. MacKay, *The Clockwork Image*, Inter-Varsity Press 1974.

14. Donald M. MacKay, *Science, Chance and Providence*, Oxford University Press 1978, p. 33.

15. Schoffeniels, op. cit.

16. Ibid., p. 108.

17. Ibid., p. 16.

18. See, for example, G. Nicolis and I. Prigogine, *Self-Organization in Nonequilibrium Systems*, Wiley-Interscience, New York 1977.

19. Schoffeniels, op. cit., p. 27.

20. M. Eigen, 'Self-organization of Matter and the Evolution of Biological Macromolecules', *Naturwissenschaften*, 58, 1971, p. 465–523.

21. Hugo Meynell, 'Monod's Muddle', *The Month*, July 1973, pp. 241–243.

22. Ibid., p. 242.

23. Ibid., p. 243.

24. J. Lewis, op. cit.

25. Donald M. MacKay, *The Clockwork Image*, Chapter 4.
26. Mary Hesse, 'On the Alleged Incompatibility between Christianity and Science', *Man and Nature*, ed. Hugh Montefiore, Collins 1975, pp. 121–131.
27. A. R. Peacocke, op. cit.
28. Paul C. W. Davies, *The Accidental Universe*, Cambridge University Press 1982.
29. William G. Pollard, *Chance and Providence*, Scribner, New York 1958, Faber & Faber 1959.
30. A. R. Peacocke, 'Chance, Potentiality and God', *Beyond Chance and Necessity*, pp. 13–25.
31. A. R. Peacocke, *Science and the Christian Experiment*, Oxford University Press 1971.
32. A. R. Peacocke, *Creation and the World of Science*.
33. Ibid., p. 94.
34. Ibid., pp. 97–103.
35. Manfred Eigen and Ruthild Winkler, *Laws of the Game*, Allen Lane, Penguin Books 1982. First published as *Das Spiel: Naturgesetze steuern den Zufall*, R. Piper Verlag, Munich 1975.
36. M. Eigen, op. cit., p. 519.

3. God or Chance

1. John Hick, *Arguments for the Existence of God*, Macmillan 1970, p. 14. The argument is taken from Le Comte du Noüy, *Human Destiny*, Longmans Green and Co., New York 1947, Chapter 3.
2. Wallace I. Matson, *The Existence of God*, Cornell University Press, Ithaca, New York 1965. Matson also noted the inappropriateness of du Noüy's calculation.
3. John Arbuthnot, 'An argument for a Divine Providence, taken from the constant Regularity observ'd in the Births of both Sexes', *Philosophical Transactions of the Royal Society*, No. 328, 1710, p. 186.
4. A. J. Ayer, *Part of My Life*, Collins 1977, p. 209.
5. Paul C. W. Davies, 'Chance or Choice: is the Universe an Accident?', *New Scientist*, 16, November 1978, pp. 506–508.
6. Le Comte du Noüy, op. cit.
7. Fred Hoyle and Chandra Wickramasinghe, *Evolution from Space*, Dent 1981.
8. *Methodist Recorder*, 27 August 1981.
9. Le Comte du Noüy, op. cit., Chapter 3.
10. Hoyle and Wickramasinghe, op. cit., p. 24.
11. Hick, op. cit., pp. 16, 17.
12. M. Eigen, 'Self-organization of Matter and the Evolution of Biological Macromolecules', *Naturwissenschaften*, 58, 1971, pp. 519.
13. G. Nicolis and I. Prigogine, *Self-organization in Nonequilibrium Systems*, Wiley-Interscience, New York 1977.
14. D. A. Gillies, *An Objective Theory of Probability*, Methuen 1973.
15. Davies, op. cit.
16. Ayer, op. cit., p. 209.
17. Alister Hardy, Robert Harvie and Arthur Koestler, *The Challenge of*

Chance, Hutchinson 1973.

18. The approach is commonly termed 'Bayesian' after Thomas Bayes (1702–1761), a Presbyterian minister in Tunbridge Wells. He proved a celebrated theorem which is central to the approach. The demonstration that subjective probabilities can be handled rigorously is of much later date and largely rests on the work of Leonard J. Savage, *The Foundations of Statistics*, Wiley, New York 1954 and Bruno de Finetti, *Theory of Probability* (Vols I and II), Wiley, New York Vol. I, 1974; Vol. II, 1975.

19. Hoyle and Wickramasinghe, op. cit., p. 130.

20. Some of the most recent work in probability *is* concerned with what subjective probabilities *ought* to be. This derives from the fact that if we look at all those events or propositions to which an individual assigns probability 0.3 then we should expect about 30% of them to occur (or be true). By this means we can, in principle, determine whether a person makes good probability judgments. The probability judgments of such 'well-calibrated' people on the question of God's existence should then be treated with some respect. However, the vast and varied nature of the evidence raises very serious questions about the propriety of reasoning in this way.

21. Hoyle and Wickramasinghe, op. cit., p. 24.

22. The implications of this statement require deeper investigation. One might well feel that, in the last resort, there ought to be only one random hypothesis, this being a description of what would have happened in the absence of any purposive direction whatsoever. The practical problem is that the randomness in the model has to embrace our ignorance about the processes involved as well as the pure randomness. Thus, when calculating the probabilities of forming enzymes from amino acids we might accord all combinations equal probability on the grounds that we have no knowledge about the nature of the process to enable us to do otherwise. If, however, such knowledge becomes available the area of uncertainty will be reduced and a different chance model will apply. In allowing a collection of possible random hypotheses we are, in effect, allowing for the fact that our knowledge of the process is incomplete.

23. D. H. Mellor, 'God and Probability', *God, Man and Religion*, ed. K. E. Yandell, McGraw-Hill, New York 1973, pp. 472–481. Reprinted in revised form from *Religious Studies*, 5, pp. 223–234.

24. Richard Swinburne, *The Existence of God*, Clarendon Press 1979.

25. Mellor, op. cit., p. 481.

26. Swinburne, op. cit., the use made of Bayes theorem is in the section beginning on p. 64.

27. P. C. W. Davies, *The Accidental Universe*, Cambridge University Press 1982.

4. *Chance and Certainty*

1. As stated this definition is concerned with events and not, for example, with uncertainty with regard to the truth of propositions. The latter is a legitimate concern of probability theory but the more restricted view is sufficient for our purposes.

2. Karl Popper, *The Logic of Scientific Discovery*, Hutchinson 1959, third edition 1968, p. 205.

3. A. J. Ayer, 'Chance', *Scientific American*, 213. Reprinted in *Risk and Chance*, ed. J. Dowie and P. Lefrere, Open University Press 1980, p. 51.

4. Essentially the same method was used, according to the Talmud, for selecting priests for Temple duty. In this case the officer responsible announced a number much larger than the number of priests present; counting then continued round the circle until the pre-assigned number was reached. See Nachum L. Rabinovitch, *Probability and Statistical Inference in Ancient and Medieval Jewish Literature*, University of Toronto Press 1973, p. 32.

5. Donald M. MacKay, *Science, Chance and Providence*, Oxford University Press 1978, p. 27.

6. Ian Stewart, 'In Favour of Chaos', *The Guardian*, Thursday 7 January 1982, p. 11.

7. William G. Pollard, *Chance and Providence*, Scribner, New York 1958, Faber & Faber 1939, p. 74.

8. See Chapter 1, note 12, above.

9. Prince Albert, 'Address of the President as president of the 4th Session of the International Statistical Congress', *Journal of the Royal Statistical Society*, 23, pp. 280–281.

10. In a letter to Dr William Farr of the General Registry Office written in 1874 and speaking of Quetelet's work, she said 'his was the very highest kind of religion: the seeking in the Laws of the Moral World which he has done so much to discover the action or plan of Supreme Wisdom and Goodness'. Quoted in Marion Diamond and Mervyn Stone, 'Nightingale on Quetelet I', *Journal of the Royal Statistical Society*, A, 144, 1981, p. 72.

11. Much fascinating material on early views of the theological implications of the statistical regularities occurring in nature and society is to be found in Karl Pearson, *The History of Statistics in the 17th and 18th Centuries*, ed. E. S. Pearson, Charles Griffin and Co. 1978. Karl Pearson himself thought that Florence Nightingale's view that God expresses his laws through statistics led, to 'a somewhat dreary universe dominated by Calvinistic determination', op. cit., p. 161.

12. Manfred Eigen and Ruthild Winkler, *Laws of the Game*, Allen Lane, Penguin Books 1982. First published as *Das Spiel: Naturgesetze steuern den Zufall*, R. Piper Verlag, Munich 1975.

13. A detailed account of such processes is given in D. J. Bartholomew, *Stochastic Models for Social Processes*, third edition, J. Wiley and Sons 1982, Chapters 9 and 10.

14. George Zipf, *Human Behavior and the Principle of Least Effort*, Addison-Wesley, Reading, Mass. 1949.

15. S. A. Kauffman, 'Metabolic Stability and Epigenesis in Randomly Constructed Genetic Nets', *Journal of Theoretical Biology*, 22, 1969, pp. 437–467.

16. Ibid., p. 466.

17. G. Nicolis and I. Prigogine, *Self-Organization in Nonequilibrium Systems*, Wiley-Interscience, New York 1977.

18. Eigen and Winkler, op. cit.

19. Kauffman, op. cit.

5. *God of Chance*

1. William G. Pollard, *Chance and Providence*, Scribner, New York 1958, Faber & Faber 1959.
2. J. D. Douglas (ed.) *The New Bible Dictionary*, Inter-Varsity Press 1962. See, for example, the article on Creation.
3. Ian G. Barbour, *Issues in Science and Religion*, SCM Press 1966, p. 298.
4. Donald M. MacKay, *Science, Chance and Providence*, Oxford University Press 1978, pp. 31ff.
5. E. Schoffeniels, *Anti-Chance*, Pergamon Press 1976, translated from the second edition of *L'Anti-Hasard*, Gauthier-Villars, first edition 1973.
6. MacKay, op. cit., pp. 33ff.
7. Hugh Meynell, 'Monod's Muddle', *The Month*, July 1973, p. 242.
8. John Hick, *Arguments for the Existence of God*, Macmillan 1970, p. 19.
9. Sir Thomas Brown, *Religio Medici*, 1672. Quotation taken from Charles Sayle (ed.), *The Works of Sir Thomas Browne*, John Grant, Edinburgh 1912, Vol. I, p. 30.
10. Ibid., p. 27.
11. Ibid., p. 29.
12. R. Hooykaas, *Religion and the Rise of Modern Science*, Scottish Academic Press 1972, p. 17.
13. A. R. Peacocke, *Creation and the World of Science*, Clarendon Press 1979. See especially Chapter 3.
14. David A. Pailin, 'God and Creation – A Process View', *Epworth Review*, January 1982, pp. 72–86.
15. Richard Swinburne, *The Coherence of Theism*, Clarendon Press 1977, p. 128, (footnote).
16. Nachum L. Rabinovitch, *Probability and Statistical Inference in Ancient and Medieval Jewish Literature*, University of Toronto Press 1973.
17. Florence N. David, *Games, Gods and Gambling*, Charles Griffin and Co. 1962.
18. Rabinovitch, op. cit., p. 34.
19. Ibid., p. 28.
20. Rabinovitch points out that the same was true in Israelite religion. 'The uneasiness which the Talmudic sages felt about the reliability of lots as expressing the Divine will is poignantly expressed in the argument ascribed to Achan confronting Joshua: "Joshua, do you want to charge me by a lot? You and Eleazor the priest are the two greatest men of the generation, yet were I to cast lots upon you, it must needs fall on one of you!" Thus it is clear that in the absence of evidence of heavenly sanction the outcome of the lot was considered to be pure chance.' Ibid., p. 23.
21. John Macquarrie, *Principles of Christian Theology* (revised ed.) SCM Press 1977, pp. 239f.
22. The quotations are from Thomas Aquinas, *Summa Contra Gentiles* literally translated by the English Dominican Fathers, Burns, Oates and Washbourne, Book II 1923, p. 86; Book III 1928. Chapter LXXIV p. 183.
23. *A Directory for the Publique Worship of God*, Printed for the Company of Stationers London 1645. pp. 65f.
24. *The New Whole Duty of Man, Containing The Faith as well as Practice of*

A Christian, (anon) W. Bent, London 1821, p. 75.

25. Alexander Pope, *Essay on Man*. Quoted from Maynard Mack (ed.) *An Essay on Man*, Methuen 1950, Epistle I, lines 289–292. See also Epistle IV, line 113.

> God sends not ill: if rightly understood
> Or partial ill is universal Good.

26. G. D. Yarnold, *Christianity and Physical Science*, A. R. Mowbray and Co. 1950, pp. 100f.

27. Florence N. David, *Games, Gods and Gambling*, Charles Griffin and Co. 1962, p. 14.

28. Rupert Davies and Gordon Rupp, (eds), *A History of the Methodist Church in Great Britain*, Vol. I, Epworth Press 1965, p. 52.

29. John Telford, *The Life of the Rev. Charles Wesley, M.A..*, Wesleyan Methodist Book Room 1900, p. 46.

30. John T. Wilkinson, 'The Rise of Other Methodist Traditions', *A History of the Methodist Church in Great Britain*, Vol. II, R. Davies, A. Raymond George and G. Rupp (eds), Epworth Press 1978, p. 279. The matter is in the Minutes of Conference for 1792.

31. Article by 'Didymus', *The Wesleyan Methodist Magazine*, 1828, pp. 596–602.

32. Orland Gingerich, *The Amish of Canada*, Herald Press, Kitchener, Ontario (no date), p. 218. Originally published by Conrad Press, Waterloo, Ontario.

33. Mary Baker Eddy, *Science and Health with Key to the Scriptures*. The trustees under the will of Mary Baker G. Eddy, Boston, USA 1875, p. 424.

34. 'Challenging Chance and Accidents', *Christian Science Monitor*, 11 October 1982.

35. Alister Hardy, Robert Harvie and Arthur Koestler, *The Challenge of Chance*, Hutchinson 1973.

36. Arthur Koestler, *The Roots of Coincidence*, Pan Books 1974. First published by Hutchinson 1972.

37. Hardy, Harvie and Koestler, op. cit., pp. 196f.

38. These are two standard sets of statistical tables containing random numbers which Hardy and Harvie used in their experiments.

6. *Chance and Providence*

1. Michael J. Langford, *Providence*, SCM Press 1981. The three heads are the last in a list of six given on p. 6. The first three are: the creative activity of God, the sustaining activity of God and God's action as final cause. They are listed in order of increasing involvement of God in the created order.

2. Alexander Pope, *Essay on Man*, Epistle I in Maynard Mack (ed.), *An Essay on Man*, Methuen 1950, lines 289–292.

3. Langford, op. cit., p.79.

4. Arthur Koestler, *The Roots of Coincidence*, Pan Books 1974 first published by Hutchinson 1972, pp. 88–90.

5. E. Schoffeniels, *Anti-Chance. A reply to Monod's Chance and Necessity*, Pergamon Press 1976. Translated by B. L. Reid from the second edition of *L'Anti-Hasard*, Gauthier-Villars, first edition 1973.

6. Thomas Aquinas, *Summa Contra Gentiles* literally translated by the English Dominican Fathers, Burns, Oates and Washbourne Book III, 1928, Chapter LXXIV, p. 183.

7. William G. Pollard, *Chance and Providence*, Scribner, New York 1958, Faber & Faber 1959.

8. Langford, op. cit., p. 79.

9. Pollard, op. cit., p. 74.

10. See, for example, Ronald W. Clark, *Einstein, the Life and Times*, Hodder & Stoughton, 1973, p. 327.

11. Pollard, op. cit., p. 22.

12. After the French mathematician S. D. Poisson. Sometimes called the law of rare events it specifies the probability of 0, 1, 2, . . . occurrences in a fixed time by a simple formula depending only on the average number of occurrences.

13. Pollard, op. cit., p. 56.

14. For example, G. Nicolis and I. Prigogine, *Self-organization in Non-equilibrium Systems*, Wiley-Interscience, New York 1977.

15. Pollard, op. cit., pp. 87, 88.

16. Pope, see above note 2.

17. Peter T. Geach, *Providence and Evil*, Cambridge University Press 1977, p. 115.

18. Ibid., p. 116.

19. This appears to be the intention behind the remark (Geach, op. cit., p. 118) that 'any singular issue is compatible with any statistical regularity'. The idea behind the passage is that God designs things to happen in an apparently random way but that, on occasions, he may change his mind, for example, in answer to prayer. This can be done without any detectable disturbance to the established statistical regularities. A similar idea seems to be implicit in Mary Hesse, ('On the Alleged Incompatibility between Christianity and Science', *Man and Nature*, ed., Hugh Montefiore, Collins 1975, p. 128) when she speaks of the 'hypothesis according to which God is active to direct the course of evolution at points that look random from the purely scientific point of view'. However, no single event can 'look random'. Randomness is a property of collections of events, but if God did intervene the isolated case would not constitute a detectable departure from the overall randomness of such events.

20. A. R. Peacocke, *Creation and the World of Science*, Clarendon Press 1979. Pollard's work is discussed on pp. 95ff. The discussion of models of God's way of acting is in Chapter 4, section IV.

21. Ian G. Barbour, *Myths, Models and Paradigms*, SCM Press 1974.

22. See, for example, Maurice Wiles, 'Farrer's Concept of Double Agency', *Theology*, July 1981, p. 243 and David Galilee, Brian Hebblethwaite, Maurice Wiles, 'Farrer's Concept of Double Agency', *Theology*, January 1982, p. 7. The antecedents of the debate and further references are given in these two articles.

23. The claim was made by Helmut Schmidt in a BBC Horizon programme on 26 September 1983. An experiment was shown in which a set of bulbs were placed round the perimeter of a circle. One bulb was illuminated at any time. At each step the illuminated bulb was switched off and one of its neighbours came on. The timing of the change and the choice of the direction of movement were determined by the random emissions of radio-active particles

in such a way that clockwise and anti-clockwise steps were equally likely. Left to itself there would thus be no discernable tendency for the light to 'rotate' in one direction rather than the other. A subject was then asked to 'will' the light to move clockwise, say. It was claimed that there was a small but statistically significant effect in the desired direction and that this had been replicated in many laboratories. The implication was that mind could influence 'chance' outcomes in a desired direction.

7. Chance and Theology

1. Julius Lipner, 'Theology and Religious Studies: Thoughts on a Crisis of Identity', *Theology*, May 1983, p. 201.

2. Peter T. Geach, *Providence and Evil*, Cambridge University Press 1977, Chapter 1.

3. John B. Cobb Jr and David R. Griffin, *Process Theology: An Introductory Exposition*, Christian Journals, Belfast 1977.

4. A. R. Peacocke, *Creation and the World of Science*, Clarendon Press 1979, p. 141.

5. In addition to the two arguments on the matter outlined here there is also the point that if extra-terrestrial life did exist, we might expect it to have contacted us by now. This argument that we are alone has been put by Frank Tipler in the *Quarterly Journal of the Royal Astronomical Society*, 21, September 1980, pp. 267–281.

6. The question of how to reconcile the uniqueness of Christ with the randomness of the processes which generate life is raised in John A. T. Robinson, *The Human Face of God*, SCM Press 1973, p. 66.

7. Martin Cressey, 'The Ordination of Women: Theological and Biblical Issues', *Epworth Review*, 10, No. 3 1983, p. 63.

8. Richard Swinburne, *The Existence of God*, Clarendon Press 1979, Chapter 11.

9. Swinburne, op. cit., p. 202.

10. The *Book of Common Prayer* is a partial exception with prayers relating to fair weather, rain, death and famine.

11. Pierre Teilhard de Chardin, *The Phenomenon of Man*, Collins 1955, Chapter 11.

INDEX